Fortress • 47

Fortifications of the Incas

1200–1531

H W & J E Kaufmann • Illustrated by Adam Hook

Series editors Marcus Cowper and Nikolai Bogdanovic

First published in 2006 by Osprey Publishing
Midland House, West Way, Botley, Oxford OX2 0PH, UK
443 Park Avenue South, New York, NY 10016, USA
E-mail: info@ospreypublishing.com

ISBN 10: 1 84176 939 8
ISBN 13: 978 1 84176 939 4

Cartography: Map Studio, Romsey, UK
Typeset in Monotype Gill Sans and ITC Stone Serif
Design: Ken Vail Graphic Design, Cambridge, UK
Index by Glyn Sutcliffe
Originated by United Graphics, Singapore
Printed in China through Bookbuilders

06 07 08 09 10   10 9 8 7 6 5 4 3 2 1

A CIP catalog record for this book is available from the British Library.

FOR A CATALOG OF ALL BOOKS PUBLISHED BY OSPREY MILITARY AND AVIATION PLEASE CONTACT:

Osprey Direct, c/o Random House Distribution Center, 400 Hahn Road, Westminster, MD 21157
Email: info@ospreydirect.com

Osprey Direct UK, P.O. Box 140, Wellingborough, Northants, NN8 2FA, UK
E-mail: info@ospreydirect.co.uk

www.ospreypublishing.com

Image credits

Unless otherwise stated, the photographic images that appear in this work were taken by the authors.

Artist's note

Readers may care to note that the original paintings from which the color plates in this book were prepared are available for private sale. All reproduction copyright whatsoever is retained by the Publishers. All enquiries should be addressed to:

Scorpio Gallery
PO Box 475
Hailsham
Sussex
BN27 2SL
UK

The Publishers regret that they can enter into no correspondence upon this matter.

The Fortress Study Group (FSG)

The object of the FSG is to advance the education of the public in the study of all aspects of fortifications and their armaments, especially works constructed to mount or resist artillery. The FSG holds an annual conference in September over a long weekend with visits and evening lectures, an annual tour abroad lasting about eight days, and an annual Members' Day.
The FSG journal *FORT* is published annually, and its newsletter *Casemate* is published three times a year. Membership is international. For further details, please contact:
The Secretary, c/o 6 Lanark Place, London W9 1BS, UK

The Coast Defense Study Group (CDSG)

The Coast Defense Study Group (CDSG) is a non-profit corporation formed to promote the study of coast defenses and fortifications, primarily but not exclusively those of the United States of America; their history, architecture, technology, and strategic and tactical employment. Membership in the CDSG includes four issues of the organization's two quarterly publications, the *Coast Defense Journal* and the *CDSG Newsletter*. For more information about the CDSG please visit www.cdsg.org or to join the CDSG write to:
[Attn: Glen Williford] Coast Defense Study Group, Inc., 634 Silver Dawn Court, Zionsville, IN 46077-9088, USA

Front Cover: The Inca mountain stronghold of Machu Picchu. (Copyright of Edward Moore)

Contents

Introduction

When Francisco Pizarro and his men reached the borders of the Inca Empire in 1531, the Inca dominions had reached their maximum extent after a period of rapid expansion lasting barely 100 years. Extending from the Angesmayo River in what is today Colombia to the Maule River in present-day Chile, the Inca Empire spanned 4,000km, covered 3,000,000km^2, included 5,000km of coastline, and numbered some 12 million (and perhaps as many as 32 million) inhabitants. The Incas named their empire Tawantinsuyu, which means the "four corners of the world" in their language and called their capital Cuzco, which they considered to be the "navel of the world."

Tawantinsuyu encompassed three major climatic regions: the arid coastal plain with some of the harshest deserts on the planet, the cordillera of the Andes with high plateaus and mountain peaks reaching elevations of more than 6,600m, and the cloud-forest shrouded Montaña region on the eastern side of the Andes, at the headwaters of the Amazon and some of its tributaries. Elevation plays an important role in this region, creating a multitude of microenvironments that support a wide variety of flora and fauna. Surprisingly, civilization in this part of the world was not born on the lush slopes of the eastern Andes, but along the river valleys that irrigated the arid plains of the Pacific coast.

BELOW The Andean cordillera landscape. In the Altiplano, rainfall is sparse, and the landscape is dominated by grasses and shrubs, which provide ideal pasture for herds of llamas and alpacas. Water comes from streams fed by run-off from glaciers that blanket the higher mountain peaks. This area is also suitable for the cultivation of high-elevation crops such as potatoes.

Tawantinsuyu was divided into four major administrative provinces or *suyos*: the northwestern province of Chinchaysuyu, which extended up to the Angesmayo River, in the vicinity of Pasto, Colombia; the northeastern province of Antisuyu, which encompassed the eastern slopes of the Andes and the steamy jungles of the head waters of the Amazon and its tributaries; the southwestern province of Cuntisuyu, which comprised the coastal region of present-day Peru; and the southeastern province of Collasuyu, which included part of the territory of present-day Bolivia and part of northern Argentina.

The people of this vast empire spoke over 160 distinct languages and dialects belonging to 16 different language groups: Arauan, Arakawan, Aymaran, Cahuapanan, Harakmbet, Jivaroan, Panoan, Peba-Yaguan, Quechuan, Tacanan, Tucanoan, Tupi, Witotoan, Zaparoan, and two unspecified groups. Each language represented a distinct ethnicity and culture. To unify their vast empire, the Incas imposed their own language, Quechua, as the official language. By the time the Spanish conquistadors appeared, however, Quechua had supplanted the local languages only in those areas that had been under Inca control for a very long time.

The cultures of the people subjugated by the Incas were as varied as the rugged landscape that surrounded them. They included city

dwellers, farmers, horticulturalists, pastoralists, fishermen, and hunters and gatherers. The slopes of the eastern Andes, by the headwaters of the Amazon and its tributaries, were inhabited by tribes of headhunting horticulturalists who raised typical subtropical crops like manioc, taro, and a variety of tropical fruit, and hunted wild animals and brilliant-feathered birds. The Altiplano (high plains) were occupied by pastoralists who depended on the llama and the alpaca for their livelihood and by some farmers who adopted the crops of their neighbors; the coastal plains were home to farmers and fishermen.

In order to maintain their hold on this vast and diverse empire, the Incas had to develop an efficient administration backed by a formidable military machine. The latter included not only an impressive fighting force, but also a logistical system that relied on roads and fortifications to insure the smooth supply of troops and their deployment.

ABOVE The Pachacamac area is typical coastal plain landscape. The valley and the delta at the mouth of the river are irrigated by water coming from the snowmelt-fed stream. The lush, green fields are bounded by desert sands.

LEFT In the Montaña region, rainfall is abundant and the mountains are shrouded with lush, tropical vegetation. This area provided the Incas with tropical fruits, manioc, coca leaves, and the bright-hued plumage of parrots and other jungle birds.

THE INCA EMPIRE c.1531

COLOMBIA

Pasto

Angesmayo

Quito

ECUADOR

Tumbes

Amazon

BRAZIL

CHINCHAYSUYU

Marañón

Ucayali

Chan Chan

PERU

Urubamba

Jauja

Ollantaytambo

Machu Picchu

Pachacamac

ANTISUYU

Cuzco

CUNTISUYU

Tiahanaco

BOLIVIA

Incallacta

Chuquisaca

Porco

PACIFIC OCEAN

COLLASUYU

PARAGUAY

C H I L E

Copiago

Tingasta

Coquimbo

ARGENTINA

Curicó

Maule

—·—·— Modern country boundaries

ANTISUYU —··—··— Extent of the major four administrative regions of Tawantinsuyu, the name of the Incan empire, c.1531

Expansion of the Incan empire:
Pachacuti 1438–71
Tupa Inca 1471–93
Huayna Capac 1493–1527

——— Inca road network

N

0 ———— 250 miles

0 ———— 500km

Chronology

Pre-Inca civilizations

According to the Incas, they were the sole bearers of civilization in South America and they were given the mission of civilizing the four corners of the world by the sun god, Inti. In reality, civilization was born in the lush oases of the arid coastal planes of South America during the third millennium BCE. The oldest known urban and ceremonial center, recently discovered at Caral by Peruvian archaeologist R. Shady-Solís and her team, dates back to circa 2700 BCE. This civilization eventually spread all along the coastal region and the interior, eventually giving way to better-known civilizations like Moche and Chimú, on the northern coast, Nazca in the southern coast, Chavín on the Altiplano, and Tiwanaku around lake Titicaca. The little-known civilization of the Chachapoyas flourished to the north of Cuzco, on the mist-shrouded flanks of the eastern Andes. Thus, by the time the Incas started to make their presence known in the Cuzco valley, they were surrounded by formidable kingdoms whose roots went back for thousands of years.

BELOW LEFT The second Inca, Sinchi Roca, in an engraving by Guamán Poma de Ayala, a 17th-century chronicler of mixed Spanish-Inca ancestry,

BELOW RIGHT The ninth Inca, Pachacutec, in an engraving by Guamán Poma de Ayala.

Chronology of civilizations in pre-Colombian Peru

Dates	Coastal region		Highlands	Titicaca region	Periods
1532 onwards	Spanish				Colonial
1532 to 1438	Inca				Late
1200	Chimú	Inca	Inca	Aymara kingdoms	Late intermediate
1000	Sican		Chanca	Tiwanaku	Middle
500	Moche	Nazca	Wari or Huari		Early intermediate
250 BCE	Gallinazo		Chavin (walled urban and	Chiripa (walled urban and	
500 BCE	Salinar	Paracas	ceremonial centers)	ceremonial centers)	Early
	(walled urban and ceremonial centers)				
c. 2500 to 3000 BCE	First urban center and temple mound at Caral		Villages and irrigation	Villages and irrigation	Pre-ceramic
5000 BCE	Appearance of agriculture, village life, earliest fortified settlements known as *canchas*.				Lithic
5000 to 8000 BCE	More permanent settlements, hunting and gathering, fishing on the coast.				
10,000 to 30,000 BCE	First evidence of human settlement in Peru – big-game hunting, gathering, fishing.				Paleo-Indian

The Inca dynasty

The origins of the Incas are shrouded in mystery, since it is not known precisely where they came from and how long ago they entered the Cuzco Valley. What is known, however, is that they were Quechua speakers. The term "Inca" does not refer to a nationality or a language; it was, instead, a title assumed by the rulers of a clan that traced its ancestry to Manco Capac, a mythical man who came, full-grown, out of a cave. In time, the term Inca came to refer to the entire ruling class of Cuzco. The name of their land, however, was Tawantinsuyu, or "Four corners of the world."

The history of the Inca dynasty can be divided into three major periods: the lordship of Cuzco period, the imperial period, and the post-Spanish conquest period. During the first period, which lasted from c.AD 1200 to 1438, the Incas consolidated their hold on the city of Cuzco and subjugated the entire valley, becoming a power to be reckoned with in the process. The fifth lord of Cuzco assumed the title of Inca, which means king or emperor, and forbade its use by anyone else. By the end of this period, the eighth Inca – who assumed the name of the god Viracocha – was casting his eyes beyond the sierras surrounding his valley. His successor, Pachacutec, who may not have been his son, began the conquest of the "four corners of the world," and in the process transformed the valley kingdom into an empire. His greatest contribution, however, was laying down the legal, religious, social, and military structures of the Inca empire that would enable his successor, Tupa Inca, to extend the borders of the empire from the river Maule in Chile to what is today Ecuador. Tupa Inca's son, Huayna Capac, consolidated the Incas' hold on the territories subjugated by his father and expanded the Inca conquest in the north. Although he left the administrative and religious affairs in the hands of capable relatives in Cuzco, Huayna Capac transferred his military headquarters to the area of Quito, where he established his main residence. When he died of smallpox in 1527, he was in no condition to appoint a definite successor, as was the custom.

Huayna Capac's oldest son, Huascar, who had spent his life in Cuzco, seized power in the capital. However, Huayna Capac's favorite son Atahualpa, who had spent his youth at his side and taken over the reins of the Inca armies in the north, refused to travel to Cuzco to swear his allegiance to his brother.

Huascar and his supporters accused him of wanting to secede and sent army after army to bring him to his knees. After a bloody war that lasted five years, Callcochima and Quiz-Quiz, Atahualpa's seasoned generals, defeated Huascar, took him prisoner, triumphantly entered Cuzco, and savagely exterminated all suspected Huascar supporters and their entire lineages. Huascar was dragged north to Atahualpa's capital to face an ignominious death. In the meantime, on November 16, 1532 Atahualpa fell into the clutches of Francisco Pizarro and his small band of conquistadors at Cajamarca. The Spaniard promised his release in exchange for a roomful of gold and a roomful of silver. While he was imprisoned, Atahualpa ordered his generals to murder Huascar so the Spaniards would not be tempted to replace him on the Cuzco throne. When Atahualpa's ransom was finally delivered, Pizarro gave the hapless Inca the choice of being burned at the stake, or converting to Christianity and being garrotted instead. Atahualpa chose to be garrotted in order to save his immortal soul. He died in 1533.

The Spaniards installed another son of Huayna Capac on the Cuzco throne, but he was promptly poisoned. His brother and successor, Manco Inca, turned against the Spanish conquistadors and took refuge in the jungle-shrouded fastness of Vilcabamba. He was succeeded by his sons, Sayri Tupa Inca, Titu Cusi, and Tupac Amaru, who was captured by the Spaniards and executed in 1572. At the same time as Manco Inca and his sons were holding out in their mountain kingdom, Paullu Inca, another son of Huayna Capac, continued to rule in Cuzco as a puppet Inca, until he was replaced by a viceroy appointed by the King of Spain and his descendants intermingled with the Spanish ruling class of Peru.

Chronology of the Incas

Estimated dates	Ruler	Accomplishments
Incas after the Spanish conquest		
1571–1572	Tupac Amaru	Third son of Manco Inca. Was captured and executed by the Spanish viceroy.
1558–1571	Titu Cusi	Second son of Manco Inca. Continued the Inca resistance in Vilcabamba (see Manco Inca below).
1545–1558	Sayri Tupa Inca	First son of Manco Inca. Succeeded Manco Inca in the Inca Vilcabamba state.
1549–1572	Carlos Inca	Son of Paullu Inca. Puppet Inca in Cuzco, who married a Spanish lady.
1536–1549	Paullu Inca	Son of Huayna Capac. Chosen to replace Manco Inca by the Spaniards, helped the Spanish to establish their hold on Tawantinsuyu.
1533–1545	Manco Inca	Son of Huayna Capac. Crowned by the Spaniards, rebelled in 1536, and established an independent jungle state in the Vilcabamba region, on the eastern slopes of the Andes (in Antisuyu).
1533–1533	Tupa Haullpa	Son of Huayna Capac. Was installed on the Cuzco throne by the Spaniards. Probably died of poisoning.
Emperors of Tawantinsuyu		
1532–1533	Atahualpa	Son of Huayna Capac. Before he could reach Cuzco to assume power, he was captured and executed by Francisco Pizarro in Cajamarca.
1527–1532	Huascar	Son of Huayna Capac. After a bitter civil war, was captured and executed by his half-brother, Atahualpa.

1493–1527	Huayna Capac	Son of Tupa Inca. Expanded the empire northward to the region of Quito; died of smallpox without designating a definitive heir.
1471–1493	Tupa Inca	Son of Pachacutec. Extended the Inca dominions throughout Chile in the south and to Ecuador in the north. Some consider him to be the "Alexander the Great" of South America.
1438–1471	Pachacutec	Although he claimed to be the son of Viracocha, he may have belonged to a Hanan Cuzco moiety. Extended the Inca Empire to the coastal plain; founded Tawantinsuyu; established many of the administrative, legal, and religious systems of the empire; and organized the Inca army.
Lords of Cuzco		
1410–1438	Viracocha	Son of Yahuar Huacac. Extended Inca dominion beyond the Cuzco Valley.
1380–1410	Yahuar Huacac	Son of Inca Roca. Cemented relations with neighboring tribes through marriage; said to have been kidnapped as a child.
1350–1380	Inca Roca	Son of Capac Yupanqui. First to use the title of "Inca"; founded a school for the boys of the royal clan.
1320–1350	Capac Yupanqui	Son of Mayta Capac. First to exact tribute from tribes beyond the Cuzco Valley.
1300–1320	Mayta Capac	Son of Lloque Yupanqui. Earned a heroic reputation as a warrior; brought most of the Cuzco Valley under Inca rule.
1260–1300	Lloque Yupanqui	Son of Sinchi Roca. Began the conquest of the Cuzco Valley.
1230–1260	Sinchi Roca	Son of Manco Capac. Established his people in Cuzco.
1200–1230	Manco Capac	Mythical founder of the Inca dynasty. Claimed to be the "son of the sun"; entered the Cuzco valley.

A defensive gateway along the access trail leading to the Inca site at Ollantaytambo. Trapezoidal windows and doorways were typical of Inca construction.

Inca military infrastructure

As archaeologist Steve Leblanc has pointed out, until recently, many archaeologists have tended to ignore the role of armed conflict in their interpretations of the past, failing to look for evidence of fortification and defences in their excavation. However, the evidence is quite stark, if one only cares to look for it. It is found in the layout of the individual family compounds surrounded by a high wall and accessed through a narrow entrance that have dotted the countryside from time immemorial. It is also found in rectangular or trapezoidal walls of the pre-Inca cities like Chan-Chan and the massive walls, bastions, and towers of the Chachapoya cities of Kuelap and Vira-Vira. The historical records, such as Juan de Betanzo's *Suma y narración de los incas*, also confirm the existence of fortified sites, many of them built by the Incas.

The *cancha*

The *cancha* can be considered the oldest form of fortification in the Andean region. Many early, pre-ceramic settlements show a similar layout, starting in 5000 BCE. Clay models of *canchas* were also found in tombs of the Moche period, from around AD 500. Settlements in the late pre-Inca and early Inca period appear to have followed a similar pattern.

The *cancha* was either a square, rectangular, or trapezoidal walled compound enclosing one or more huts. It was usually accessed through a single, narrow, easily defended entrance. Its construction material varied from region to region. On the coast, the preferred materials were adobe or unbaked clay bricks. In the highlands, uncut fieldstone was the preferred building material because it was readily available and much more durable than adobe or unbaked brick. The thatch-roofed living quarters, sheds, and granaries were lined up against the four interior walls of the enclosure, surrounding a central courtyard where the family pursued its daily chores, such as weaving and processing the harvests. Cooking was usually done within the habitation hut, where the entire family shared the sleeping quarters with guinea pigs, which eventually ended up in the cooking pot, and dogs, which sounded the alarm when unexpected visitors approached the compound. The *cancha* was often surrounded by stonewalled corrals where the family's prized llamas and alpacas were penned and by terraced fields where the family grew maize, quinoa, and potatoes.

Since the sierra was singularly devoid of major predators like the jaguar and the wolf, the walled compound was clearly meant to keep out human intruders. During the reign of the first Incas, war between the various groups occupying the Cuzco Valley was common, consisting mostly of clashes between raiding warriors. According to Inca oral tradition, the victors laid to waste the homes of

BELOW This engraving by Guamán Poma de Ayala shows two rows of *colcas* (warehouses), Tupa Inca Yupanqui (1471–93), and a *quipucamayoc* (keeper of the *quipu*) – an official in charge of collecting the goods from the local community and record keeping.

the defeated, killed all the males, young and old, the women with children and those that were pregnant, and carried off the untouched females together with the livestock. In the circumstances, the fortified compound was a necessity, allowing its occupants to fend off unexpected raids.

By the time the Incas appeared in the Cuzco Valley, many of its inhabitants had also sought safety in numbers. Small hamlets, villages, and even towns dotted the slopes of the valley and two towns guarded access to the valley, up river and downriver. When two or more families lived close together, the *canchas* were built back to back so that they shared walls, but each kept a separate entrance and courtyard. In larger settlements, the *canchas* were arranged in a similar fashion, creating symmetrical blocks of walled courtyards. As a result, the pre-Colombian cities of the Andes presented a square or trapezoidal outline with a regular grid of streets and city blocks. In mountainous areas like the Cuzco Valley, the shape of the blocks was determined by the terrain, but they retained the arrangement of a central courtyard surrounded by buildings. In Cuzco, the walls of the *canchas* towered over the narrow streets, assuring the privacy of the families they sheltered. The simple pattern of the *cancha* was repeated in the layout of the Incas' palaces, temples, fortresses, and *tambos* (rest stops).

The means of communication: roads and bridges

Inca roads

Even though the Incas did not have a recognizable writing system, they were able to communicate with the most remote corners of their empire with astounding rapidity. Communication was conducted via an elaborate system of roads and bridges, runners carrying messages, and *quipucamayocs* (*quipu* keepers) able to decipher the *quipu* (an accounting method based on strings and knots; various colors, lengths, and thicknesses were knotted to represent numbers or as an aide-memoir). Thus, Francisco Pizarro's movements were duly observed and reported to Huayna Capac, Atahualpa, and Huascar almost as soon as he came within sight of their empire's borders.

By the time the Spanish conquistadors made their appearance on the northern edge of Tawantinsuyu, it is estimated that the Inca network of roads covered 40,000km, only 25,000 of which are known today. According to Father Bernabé Cobo, who actually travelled over these roads, they "were magnificent constructions, which could be compared favorably with the most superb roads of the Romans" (1979: 223). The network consisted of two main north-south highways connected by east-west transverses. These main roads were called *Capac Ñan* ("great road") in Quechua. In addition, many smaller side roads led to mountain sanctuaries, mines, and other places of interest to the Incas. Many of these roads were built over pre-existing tracks and roads used from time immemorial by the Andean people. However, unlike their predecessors, the Incas reserved the use of their roads for the movement of their troops and for the rapid transmission of messages from all corners of Tawantinsuyu to Cuzco. The transit of civilians and goods was only a second consideration.

The eastern north-south highway or sierra road ran through the Andes and Cuzco. It was divided into a northern section, called the Chinchasuyu road, and a southern section called the Collasuyu road. The Chinchasuyu road ended in the north, in the town of Huaca (today in Ecuador), passing through 28 towns of varying importance in the province of Chinchasuyu, including Anta, Limatambo, Cajamarca, Tomebamba, and Quito. At Huánuco Viejo, this road branched off to the northeast toward the territory of the Chachapoyas (Kauffmann-Doig, 1980).

The Collasuyu road began in Cuzco and ended at the town of Curicó (in Chile today), after it linked up with the coastal highway at San Felipe (south of Coquimbo). Among the most important towns on this road was Tiahanaco, where it branched off in a southerly direction, toward the town of Porco (Kauffmann-Doig, 1980).

The sierra road intersected in Cuzco with the Antisuyu and the Cuntisuyu roads. The Antisuyu road, which linked the towns of Calca, Ollantaytambo, Machu Picchu, and Vitcos to the capital, was the shortest, but traversed a breathtaking landscape of vertiginous gorges and cloud-shrouded forests along the Urubamba and Vilcabamba river valleys. The Cuntisuyu road, which ran through the forbidding terrain of the high sierra, linked Cuzco to the coast, by way of Accha and Alca (Kauffmann-Doig, 1980).

The Incas considered the Chinchaysuyu, Collasuyu, Antisuyu, and Cuntisuyu roads as the most important of their empire, since they led to its very heart and they guarded them most jealously with military outposts.

The western north-south highway or coastal road was also an important thoroughfare and had probably been used for thousands of years before the Incas came on the scene. It followed the coast, linking the coastal valleys and cities from Tumbes to the town of Curicó (in northern Chile). It merged with the sierra road at San Felipe (Kauffmann-Doig, 1980).

Eight major east-west traverses and a number of smaller trails linked the eastern sierra road to the western coastal road, crossing the rugged peaks of the Andes. The northernmost of these roads connected Cajamarca, on the Chinchaysuyu road, to the coast. From there, it continued on to the town of Balsas and linked up with the Chachapoya branch of the sierra road at Leimebamba. The second traverse linked the coastal city of Pacasmayo to a loop of the sierra road, near the city of Chavín de Huántar. Further south, a road went from the city of Pachacamac (near Lima) to the town of Jauja, on the sierra road. Not too far down the coast from Pachacamac, the coastal road passed through Chincha and intersected with the road to Vilcashuamán via Tambo Colorado, an important warehouse center, and Haitará. Next, came the Cuntisuyu road, leading directly to Cuzco. The next major traverse was located far to the south and connected the town of Copiago to Tingasta on the Collasuyu road (Kauffmann-Doig, 1980).

The construction of the roads varied, according to the terrain. Father Cobo wrote of the coastal road:

> Through all of the level land, both fertile valleys and fields as well as desert and wasteland, the road runs in a perfectly straight line, but … in the valleys it is so narrow as to be no more than twelve to fifteen feet wide, and only two or three men on horseback can go on it abreast. [1979: 224]

In the valleys, he continues, "it was enclosed by thick mud walls which were two to three *estados* high" to prevent the marching soldiers from straying onto the adjacent fields and trampling the crops. In the desert outside the valleys, the road continued along a straight line, but its width varied and the walls gave way to fruit trees or shrubs. On the coast, where the lack of rainfall did not allow for trees to grow, the road was often obliterated by the shifting sands. However, its itinerary was marked by heavy posts or large stones set at regular intervals to prevent the traveller from straying and getting lost.

In the flat stretches of the Altiplano, the sierra road was similar to the coastal road. However, the seasonal rains tended to wash away the parts running along steep scarps, unless culverts were built. The Incas also built high retaining walls to raise the level of the road or to prevent landslides from blocking it. Where the hillsides were too steep, stairs were carved into the bedrock. These stairs did not impede the flow of traffic, since the Andean Indians had few draft animals and, therefore, no wheeled transport. Often, the road would zigzag up the steep sierras and, sometimes, pass through tunnels pierced into the mountains. On the Altiplano, where the road skirted Lake Titicaca or went through wetlands, the Incas built stone-paved causeways.

A cancha of the pre-Inca period

The *cancha* has been the basic settlement unit in the Andean region from the inception of agriculture and llama herding to post-colonial times. A tall dry-stone wall enclosed the dwellings of an extended family and some storage sheds. The family owned dogs (to guard the enclosure) and guinea pigs, which were not only pets, but also an important source of protein for the family. Other closely related families lived in nearby *canchas*. In the area between the *canchas* were wall-enclosed corrals in which the clan kept its llama and alpaca herds, which provided wool to clothe the family and trade in the market town. There were also fields where the clan grew potatoes and maize. The walls kept out not only predators but also raiding parties from other tribes or clans. To defend their *canchas*, the menfolk used bolas, slings and short clubs.

Small bridges and culverts allowed it to stay dry, even when the surrounding areas flooded during the rainy season.

Thus, as Father Cobo points out, the building and maintenance of the sierra road and the east-west traverses required more skilled labor than the coastal road. After the Spaniards occupied Tawantinsuyu, they were not able to muster the workforce necessary to maintain the Inca roads, and many sections fell into disrepair, and eventually into disuse. The sections requiring little maintenance, on the other hand, were used well into the 20th century. In fact, some parts of the roads are used to this very day by the natives of the Andes.

The Incas depended heavily on the road system they helped develop in their conquest and subjugation of the Andean people and to maintain control over their territories. Indeed, the roads served as interior lines that allowed the rapid deployment and movement of troops from one part of Tawantinsuyu to another, giving them the advantage over their enemies. In addition, the excellent condition of the roads allowed the Incas' messengers to run swiftly over their stretch of road, without hitches or accidents, thus keeping the Incas informed at all times of events in their far-flung empire.

Inca bridges

In the broken terrain of the Andes, gouged by ravines and deep river valleys, bridges were an important component of the Inca road system. Although the Incas have become associated with suspension bridges, they actually used a variety of techniques to build their bridges. It is likely, however, that the Incas did not invent these bridge-building techniques, but rather borrowed them from their predecessors in the Andean region. Like the roads, the bridges were primarily reserved for the Inca and his armies. No one else was allowed to use them without special permission.

The simplest of these structures were picket bridges, found over small streams and on wetland causeways. Culverts were also built on the causeways to prevent their flooding and in the mountains to prevent the roads from being washed away.

In wide river valleys, the Incas opted for pier bridges, like the Pachacutec Bridge in the Urubamba Valley. This bridge consists of two tower piers on each bank and a stone tower saddle in the middle of the river. The tower saddle is protected by a boulder that diverts the main force of the water and prevents erosion of the structure.

When the roads had to cross deep gorges, the Incas opted for their famous rope suspension bridges. These bridges consisted of thick grass cables anchored to boulders on each side of the gorge that bore the load. Additional cables provided handrails

BELOW In this engraving, Poma de Ayala shows "the Governor of the Roads" supervising a worker on the main road (Capac Ñan). The stone pilasters are not only milestones, but also *huacas*, or sacred places worshipped by travellers along the road.

15

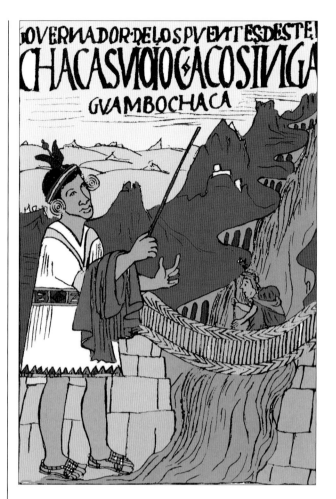

GOVERNADOR·DELOS·PVENTES·DESTE
CHACASVIOIO&ACOSINGA
GVAMBOCHACA

and supports for the decking. These bridges were strong enough to support the weight of whole units and the accompanying llamas. However, they were not very durable and had to be replaced every year. The bridge across the Apurímac River, in the vicinity of Cuzco – one of the most important during the Inca period – is still rebuilt every year by the locals.

The bridges were supervised by specially appointed officials, who were not only responsible for their maintenance, but also their security, and usage. They played an important role in the "War Between the Brothers" as armies retreated over them, strove to hold them, or burned them down to prevent their opponents from using them.

Tambos

The *tambos* were complexes that included the royal warehouses called *colcas*; an *ushnu* or temple platform, usually dedicated to Inti, the sun god; and a large habitation called a *galpon*. Father Cobo describes this as a large house with:

> only one room, one hundred to three hundred feet long and at least thirty to a maximum of fifty feet wide, all cleared and unadorned without being divided into chambers or apartments, and with two or three doors, all on one side at equal intervals. [1979: 228-9]

The *colcas* held all the necessary supplies for the Inca's soldiers: freeze-dried potatoes and meat, maize, quinoa, llama-wool blankets, warm clothing, footwear, arms, shields, helmets, and so on. The surplus was periodically taken to Cuzco where it was stored in a large complex of warehouses and redistributed by the Inca according to need and political expediency. A group of local girls called *acllas* waited hand and foot on the Inca, his dignitaries, his retinue and/or his army when they traveled.

The style of the *tambos* and the construction material varied from region to region. On the coastal plains, the favored building materials were adobe and sun-dried bricks. In the Sierra and the Altiplano, stone was preferred. The *tambos* on flat terrain tended to have trapezoidal layouts, whereas those of the highlands often had to adapt to the contours of the terrain. The size and sophistication of the complexes depended on the wealth and importance of the communities that built them.

Every village, town, and city along the roads was required to build, maintain, and supply a royal *tambo*. Additional *tambos* were built between the towns at four to five league (22–28km) intervals, which represented a day's march. *Tambos* in important strategic positions, like Ollantaytambo and Tambo Machay, tended to be heavily fortified. Others in less threatened or less important strategic positions were not. Whether fortified or not, *tambos* were of crucial importance to the Incas' armies because they constituted reliable supply points where they could assemble, rest, and reorganize as the case may be.

Chucllas and chasquis

Father Cobo wrote: "Apart from the *tambos* and storehouses along these two royal highways [the two north-south roads] every quarter of a league [c.1.25–2km] there were also some huts or small houses built in pairs facing one another near the road" (1979: 229). The appearance of the buildings and the material from which they were built varied from region to region. Some of them were no larger than a stone oven, Cobo noted. Each of these houses, called *chucllas* in Quechua, accommodated two men, so that there were a total of four at each roadside station, one pair of *chasquis* or messengers for each direction.

During the reign of the Incas, the *chucllas* were manned 24 hours a day. While one man rested or slept, the other kept watch, listening for the *chasqui* from the previous stage, who announced his approach by blowing a conch shell. At the first alert, the *chasqui* on watch jumped up and ran alongside his newly arrived colleague while receiving the oral message – the *quipu* – or package from him. He then ran to the next *chuclla* where he relayed his message in the same manner. The penalty for falling asleep while on duty was death.

Thus, messages or packages could travel as many as 50 leagues (c.275–300km) in a period of 24 hours. A message sent from Lima to Cuzco was delivered in less than two days, whereas in colonial times it took the same message 13 days to arrive (Cobo, 1979). In cases of emergency, such as uprisings, the alarm was sent by smoke signals that were relayed from hill to hill and reached the Inca long before the spoken word (Kauffmann-Doig, 1980).

The *chasquis* were selected by the local chieftains or *caciques* in childhood and trained not only to run but also to memorize messages verbatim. The penalty for modifying a message, even by one word, or divulging it to an unauthorized individual was death. They were also given a special insignia so they could be easily identified, a conch shell to announce their arrival, a bag to carry packages, and a staff to ward off wild animals. The *chasquis* occupied their *chucllas* for 15 days, rested for 15 days, and resumed their service for another fortnight. In addition to transmitting messages, they were also required to keep the records for their districts, record them on *quipus*, and send them to the capital. In return for their arduous service, the *chasquis* did not have to pay taxes in the form of labor (*mit'a*). The *chasqui* system is attributed Tupa Inca Yupanqui, the tenth Inca, who relied on it to keep an eye on his far-flung empire and ruthlessly quash any rebellion (Cobo, 1979). Thus, Francisco Pizarro and his small band of conquistadors were reported to Atahualpa in Quito before they even set foot in Tawantinsuyu and within days of crossing the borders to Huascar in Cuzco.

Pukaras

According to Juan Betanzos, during his campaigns the Inca Tupa Inca Yupanqui was struck by the fact that:

> few of the towns he had visited and subjugated lacked a stronghold or fortress where those of that town or province took refuge and defended themselves from those who wanted to harm them. [Betanzos, 1996]

He decided, therefore, to build a fortress (Sacsayhuamán) for his own capital, one that would match the city in grandeur. Apparently, he also built fortresses – called *pukaras* in Quechua – along the borders of his newly subjugated territories. According to other sources, it was his father, Pachacutec, who ordered the construction of Sacsayhuamán. Some archaeologists even suggest that the fortress pre-dated the city of Cuzco and the Inca presence in the valley (Frost, 1984).

With the exception of the large fortresses in the area of Cuzco, the structure and layout of the Inca fortresses are surprisingly uniform, which indicates that they were planned and erected by one entity in Cuzco, probably the Inca himself. The most popular sites for the *pukaras* were hilltops of pyramid shape. The walls of the *pukara* consisted of concentric terraces spiralling up the slopes of the hill to encircle a temple-storehouse-garrison complex. Since these

Capac Ñan (main road)

Roads and bridges played an important role in the Inca defensive system. They ensured the swift relay of messages between fighting units and commanders and they allowed the rapid progress of troops and supplies from recruiting points to battlefields. Both roads and bridges were built and maintained by the local communities and were the responsibility of the local *caciques*. Road and bridge building was part of the *mit'a* obligation or labor tax and was often accompanied by much dancing and drinking of *chicha*, a beer made from fermented maize. In the sierras, the roads were often hewn from the face of cliffs, or built on top of long retaining walls. In some places, tunnels were pierced through rocky outcrops. Where the gradient was too steep, the Incas carved steps in the bedrock or built stepping-stones. The suspension bridges were made with thick ropes and had to be replaced once a year. A "road and bridge governor" is shown in the lower left part of this illustration. A small unit of the Inca army armed with maces, clubs, and shields is about to cross the bridge, preceded by a running *chasqui*. Following behind the army is a train with llamas herded by children and women.

LEFT Remnants of Inca trail at Pisac. This minor road led from the Capac Ñan (main road) to the administrative-religious-military complex of Pisac. As it neared the fortified complex, the road narrowed so that the enemy was forced to approach single-file. On the steeper part of the hill, the smooth path was replaced with wide, shallow stairs.

spiralling walls resembled a snail shell, the Quechua term *churu* (snail) was sometimes incorporated into the name of the forts. Thus, the name of the *pukara* of Churuloma means "snail hill". The space behind the retaining walls of these terraces was filled with rubble and tamped soil, providing a smooth path for the defenders to move on. The rest of the bedrock between terraces was left in its natural state. The retaining wall also supported a parapet of fieldstones, which protected the defenders from enemy projectiles and allowed them to hurl stones at the attackers down the hill. Two meters-wide and four meters-deep moats were often located in front of the retaining walls of the terraces, and were filled with water if the terrain allowed it. Two-meter deep entrances pierced into the terrace walls allowed access to each level of the *pukara*. A system of stone chicanes defended the entrances to each level of the *pukara*. In some cases, small towers added extra protection (Fresco, 2005).

The complex on top of the hill was surrounded by its own wall, and if possible, a moat. It included a temple or temple platform dedicated to the sun god Inti; quarters for the commander, his troops, and a few priests; and ample storage rooms where food, clothing, and armament for the garrison were kept (Fresco, 2005). In some sites, the barracks for the garrisons were located down the slope, below the temple-palace complex.

The size of the *pukaras* and their garrisons depended on their strategic importance. Thus, Sacsayhuamán, overlooking the capital, Cuzco, was of cyclopean proportions, and was probably the largest *pukara* in the empire. One of the most important Inca forts in the area of Quito, which was well on the way to becoming the second capital of the Inca empire at the time of the War Between the Brothers, was the *pukara* of Quitoloma. On the other hand, the remote outposts on the southern border of the empire, in present-day Argentina, were more modest in size. The commander of the *pukara* was usually an *orejón* (nobleman from Cuzco) appointed by the Inca himself. The garrison, on the other hand, was usually recruited from the local population or the local *mitimacs* (Fresco, 2005).

Generally, the Inca *pukaras* stood on strategic heights overlooking the major crossroads and important settlements and *tambos*. They were built either singly or in groups of varying size, depending on the importance of the road or place they protected. Single *pukaras* were likely to guard places of lesser strategic importance, whereas groups of fortifications guarded towns and heavily travelled roads. In some places, these Inca fortifications formed successive lines of defences that ran across the valleys through which the main roads and their branches wound their way. In the north, these fortified lines usually ran from east to west to interdict passage through the valleys.

Other lines of fortification were built to guard the eastern slopes of the Andes. They ran from north to south to protect the territory of Tawantinsuyu from incursions by Amazonian tribes, or guarded the busiest roads in the region. Apparently, these lines intersected with some of the east-west lines. Fresco reports one such line on a ridge overlooking the Chinchaysuyu road: Quito-Nono-Cachillacta-Chacapata. There is some evidence of similar east-west and north-south alignments of *pukaras* in northern Argentina, at the southern end of Tawantinsuyu, but no systematic study has been carried out to definitively establish their existence.

Construction materials and techniques

One of the fields in which the Incas distinguished themselves was architecture. In this, as in every other aspect of their lives, they owed their astounding success to careful planning and administration. The construction of important structures such as temples, palaces, and *pukaras* began with the selection of the site. For the military structures, the Inca chose strategic sites overlooking roads, crossroads, the confluence of two rivers, important cities, and so on. The Inca then ordered his architects to make clay models of the structure, many of which survive to this day. Measurements were mostly anthropometrical, i.e. parts of the body, fingers, hands, arms, or legs served as the basic measure. Next, a contingent of workers was assembled at the building site and the quarry, and the work began under the supervision of the local *cacique* or chieftain. Throughout the construction, a *quipucamayoc* kept careful record of the work in progress and reported regularly to the Inca, who either approved the project or suggested modifications.

Building materials

The masons of Tawantinsuyu used a variety of building materials, depending on the natural resources available in the region where they worked. On the coast – where the rainfall was scarce, fieldstones were rare, and outcrops of suitable rock were distant – adobe and sun-baked bricks had been the material of choice since time immemorial (Hartkopf, 1985). When they conquered the

BELOW Ashlar walls at Pisac. Note that the wall is resting on the bedrock, which was carved to accommodate the first layer of stones.

RIGHT **Inca construction techniques**

The Andean Indians had few metal tools, but it appears they used either copper or bronze tools in a limited way. The bulk of work was done with stone tools and wooden stakes. Quarry sites abandoned in mid-work show that the stone cutters: **(1)** inserted hematite wedges into cracks in the bedrock and pounded them in with stone mallets, widening the cracks; **(2)** inserted wooden wedges into the cracks and poured water over them. The wet wood expanded further widening and deepening the crack. **(3)** They also freed a block from its bed by chiselling the bottom out, and propping the freed sections with piles of smaller stones. The larger stone blocks were dressed on the building site and fitted into the surrounding rocks, so they could not slide out during an earthquake. The *mitimacs* carried the stones from the quarry to the building site before they dressed them. The rough stone blocks were smoothed out with hammer stones of increasingly smaller size. The preferred rocks for this job were hard ones like obsidian or hematite. The "percussion" technique shown **(4)** left small indentations on the surface of the stones. After large stones had been dragged to the building site by gangs of *mitimacs*, they were pulled into place up a stone ramp **(5)**: once the building was complete, the ramp was removed. Cyclopean stones were pulled with ropes and propped up with rocks until their base dropped into a hole specially dug to receive them **(6)**. Sacrifices of llamas, llama foetuses and/or gold or silver llama figurines were laid under the cornerstones for good luck and prosperity.

RIGHT The cyclopean walls of Sacsayhuamán, near Cuzco. The first defensive terrace was made of these large stones measuring 9m high, 5m wide, and 4m thick.

BELOW Modern-day houses are still made of *pirca*, fieldstones and pebbles cemented with a clay-based mortar. The wall is covered with a thin layer of clay and painted white. In pre-Colombian times, many buildings were painted red and yellow.

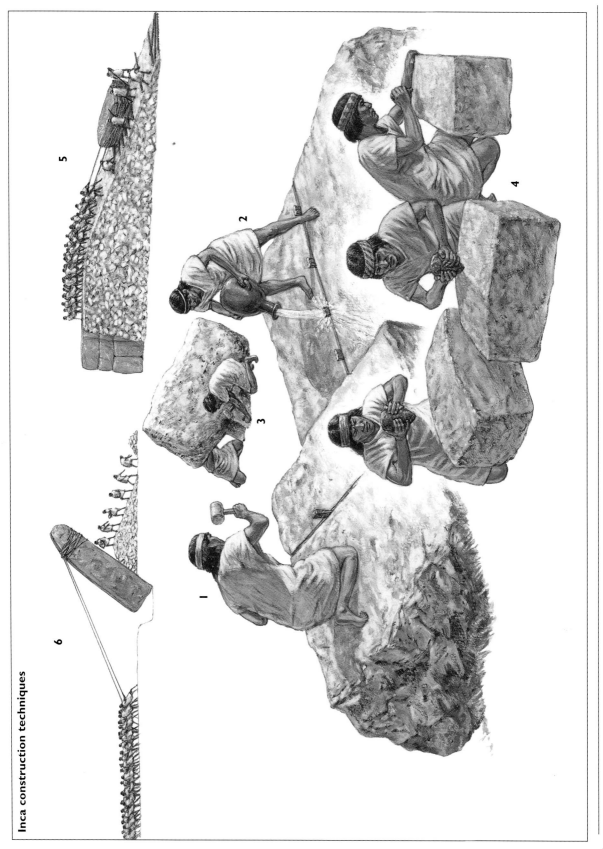

coastal regions, the Incas allowed their subjects to continue their building practices instead of imposing their own. The result was a blending of Inca design with local construction practices. Thus, the city of Tumbes was defended by snail-shaped walls made of adobe and sun-dried bricks instead of stone. The adobe and bricks were made by mixing clay with water.

In higher elevations, the Andean people had always preferred fieldstone for most of their structures because it was readily available and more durable. The practice continued into Inca times and beyond. The Incas continued to use fieldstone in the construction of structures of secondary importance, such as the border outposts, which had strictly utilitarian functions. They reserved the best building materials – cut stones – for their most important buildings: their temples, their palaces, and their most important fortresses like Sacsayhuamán. They used whatever rock was locally available, including limestone, granite, porphyry, and basalt. In most cases, the stones available to them were igneous rocks, which were very hard and difficult to work with stone tools (Kauffmann-Doig, 1980; Finch and Finch, 2005).

Doors, lintels, and rafters for the roofs were made of wood, a precious commodity in most of Tawantinsuyu, where trees were rare. The roofs were covered with thatch or palm leaves, depending on the location. Ceramic or stone tiles were not used in roofing until the colonial period, when they were introduced by the Spaniards (Kaufmann Doig, 1980; Finch and Finch, 2005).

Quarrying and transportation

Whenever possible, a suitable quarry was selected in the vicinity of the building site in order to facilitate and expedite the transportation of the stone. In some cases, however, the nearest outcrop of suitable stone was several kilometers away. For instance, the stone for the fortified administrative and religious center of Ollantaytambo had to come from across the Urubamba River valley: the stone had to be carried down into the river valley, across the wide river, and up the steep slope to the building site. No mean achievement, considering the fact that llamas can carry loads of no more than 30–40kg, and given the absence of any other draught animals and wheeled transport (Kauffmann-Doig, 1980; Finch and Finch, 2005).

In the absence of metals stronger than copper and bronze, Andean stonecutters used other techniques to cut and prepare the building stones. In some cases, they drove wooden wedges into fissures in the rock and then poured water on the wood to make it expand and split the rock. If a landslide talus was available, as in the Ollantaytambo quarry, they simply collected the rocks best suited for their purposes (Finch and Finch, 2005; Kauffmann-Doig, 1980).

Once they had separated the blocks of stone from the bedrock, the stonecutters shaped them with hammer stones. To smooth the surface of the stone blocks, they used increasingly smaller hammer stones of black obsidian, which left characteristic peck marks or percussion marks. The stonecutters prepared four different types of stone blocks: ashlars, cellular blocks, multi-cornered blocks, and cyclopean blocks.

When a large stone block was ready, a gang of workers wound a rope around it several times and pulled it to the construction site. Often, the path before the stone block was coated with mud so it could slide more easily. An engraving by Guamán Poma de Ayala, a *mestizo* (mixed race) chronicler of the 17th century, shows such a gang pulling a large rock with a whip-wielding supervisor standing on top. This method was probably used in the transportation of very large stones for the cyclopean walls of Sacsayhuamán, Ollantaytambo, and Tambo Machay (Finch and Finch, 2005; Kauffmann-Doig, 1980). Sometimes, the stonecutters carved rings on the sides of the blocks or holes in the corners, using a pestle and grit. When it came to transporting the stone to the construction site, a rope was threaded through the ring or hole before the gang of workers started pulling.

Building techniques

Andean masons used a variety of techniques to build walls. On the coast, they mixed clay and sand with water and used the mixture to shape walls. They often laid an Andean grass called *ichu* longitudinally in the clay mixture to strengthen the walls. If they used sun-dried bricks, they placed the *ichu* longitudinally in the blocks. When they built the walls, they used a clay mixture as mortar. Often, the adobe or brick walls were erected over stone foundations. The walls were thicker at the bottom and gradually tapered off toward the top. They were also battered, i.e. they leaned slightly toward the inside of the structure. It is believed that this characteristic made them more resistant to earthquakes (Kaufmann Doig, 1980; Hartkopf, 1985).

In the highlands, the Indians used the dry-wall technique to build the retaining walls for their agricultural terraces, the *pukara* terraces, and roads. Sometimes, they also used it to build their houses. They also used a technique called *pirca*, which consisted of cementing the fieldstones with a clay-based mortar mixed with pebbles. Many of the *pukaras* on the northern frontier of the Inca Empire and *tambos* on the Inca roads were made with *pirca*, which remained in use throughout the colonial period and survives to this very day in the rural areas of the Andes (Kaufmann Doig, 1980; Finch and Finch, 2005).

Like the adobe walls, the fieldstone walls were thicker at the bottom, thinner, and battered, which gave them stability, an important feature in a region plagued with earthquakes. The plasticity of the clay in the *pirca* is thought to contribute to the strength of the walls. The characteristic trapezoidal doorways and windows of the Incas added further stability to the structure. Sometimes, the *pirca* walls stood on foundations of larger, polygonal stones.

In general, however, the Incas reserved their most sophisticated building techniques for their most prized monuments like the *Coricancha* (temple of the Sun) in Cuzco, some of the imperial palaces, or the fortress of Sacsayhuamán. At these sites, many of the walls consisted of cyclopean blocks of stone

BELOW Adobe was the preferred construction material on the coastal plain. The city of Chan Chan, capital of the Chimú empire, was entirely built of adobe, including its surrounding walls. When the Incas conquered the coast, they allowed the locals to continue building in their time-honored tradition, instead of imposing highland construction techniques upon them.

BELOW LEFT Moving large stones. This 17th-century engraving by Guamán Poma de Ayala shows how large stones were transported from the quarry to the building site. The *mitimacs* (taxpayers) wound a sturdy rope around the rock and pulled with all their might while their supervisor urged them on with words – and a stick. It is reported that the path under the rock was lined with wet clay so the rock could slide more easily along the way. In 1536, when the power of the Incas collapsed, many such stones were left strewn midway between the building sites and the quarry. They are known as *piedras cansadas* or "tired stones" in Peru.

BELOW RIGHT Building a *pukara*. This engraving by Guamán Poma de Ayala shows two *orejones* (Inca noblemen) laying stones on a wall. In reality, the work was done by *mitimacs* and supervised by members of the upper class, such as the two shown here. This engraving probably represents a ceremonial laying of the bricks to bring the blessing of the gods upon the site.

anchored to each other and to the bedrock by scribing and coping, a technique frequently used in other parts of the world to build log structures. Once the cut stone arrived from the quarry, it was suspended over the bedrock on which it was to sit. The outline of the suspended blocks was traced on the bedrock with the help of a scribing device, probably a wooden triangular contraption, one point of which was moved along the underlying rock. Next, the bedrock was carved out precisely to fit the bottom of the suspended block. Finally, the block was lowered, fitting perfectly in its seat in the bedrock. The same procedure was repeated to fit the next block not only into the bedrock, but also to the side of the first block. This procedure, which worked well for medium-sized blocks, could present a real challenge in the case of the cyclopean blocks, which allowed little room for error. These enormous blocks were propped up either with stones or on a stone ramp while the masons prepared their seat. These blocks of rock can still be seen on their props and ramps at Ollantaytambo where the masons seem to have abandoned them in mid-work, probably in the wake of Atahualpa or Huascar's demise. Once they were tipped into position, these blocks would have been well nigh impossible to lift or displace (Finch and Finch: 3, 2005).

The Andean masons also anchored medium-sized blocks to each other by carving special grooves on the side of the stone blocks, placing them flush with another similarly carved block, and pouring hot metal – either copper or bronze – into the mould thus created. This allowed the wall to sway, yet remain in place during a quake. The masons also carved bosses and pits into medium rocks and ashlars and carefully fitted the bosses into the pits. They also used a thin layer of clay as a sealant. Once they finished, their walls were ready to withstand the ravages of time, weather, and seismic activity. Only the depredations of the Spaniards, who used the stone blocks to build their own houses and monuments, significantly damaged the Inca masonry.

Organization of the empire

The Incas owed their extraordinary military successes in large part to their remarkably efficient social and administrative organization. However, as in other aspects of their culture, they were not so much revolutionaries as reorganizers and innovators. Thus, they adapted pre-existing social structures, norms, and traditions to fit their needs.

Ayllus

The basic kinship unit of the Andean Indians was the nuclear family, consisting of mother, father, and their offspring. These families formed closely related lineages that could trace their origin to a common known ancestor, which, in turn, formed *ayllus* or clans that traced their ancestry to one common mythical ancestor. These social units were bound closely together by ties of mutual reciprocity. A family could always count on its lineage for help at planting and harvest time as well as in cases of emergency. When it became time to work on more ambitious projects, such as the construction of irrigation ditches or planting terraces, the lineage could always count on the help of the other lineages of the *ayllu*. The help was always reciprocal, and if a man and his family lent a hand to his neighbor and kinsman, he could and did expect help in return. In exchange, he was expected to provide food, drink, and sometimes gifts, to all the helpers (Moseley, 1992).

BOTTOM LEFT In this engraving, Guamán Poma de Ayala shows the Inca surrounded by his council consisting of his kinsmen and members of the royal *panacas*.

BOTTOM RIGHT The *colcacamayoc* or "keeper of the storehouses" was responsible for collecting goods and services from his constituents and accounting to the Sapa Inca in Cuzco. Goods were stored in the local storehouse to be redistributed to the locals. Surplus goods were reserved for the Inca's armies. When new supplies came in, the excess was sent to Cuzco.

TOP LEFT The *quipucamayoc* or "keeper of the *quipu*" had a pivotal role in the administration of Tawantinsuyu. He was trained as a young boy in the code of the *quipu*, a set of knotted strings of various colors, lengths, and thicknesses. The early Spanish colonists reported that there were various types of *quipu*. Some *quipus* held the historical record of the Inca dynasty; others held population data, including the number of possible conscripts available in each district; others still recorded the agricultural production of each district, and similar information.

TOP RIGHT A *cacique* and his *ayllu* are on their way to deliver the *mit'a* to the Inca. The clansmen carry him on their shoulders to show respect. Higher-status individuals were carried on litters.

The leader of the *ayllu*, called *curaca* or *cacique*, did not hold a hereditary position, except, perhaps, in the city-states. He was chosen from among the more experienced and respected men of the various lineages. The more relatives a man had, the more likely he was to be selected, since he could commandeer the largest work force and be of most use to the community and/or the Inca. The *curaca* resolved disputes between lineages, allocated agricultural plots to the individual families of the *ayllu*, and helped plan and supervise major construction projects that benefited all the lineages under his leadership. Related *ayllus* formed larger units such as tribes, paramount chiefdoms led by *capacs*, or kingdoms led by *sinchis*. All the *ayllus* in the chiefdoms or kingdoms were generally grouped into two corporate entities called moieties: *hanan* (upper) and *hurin* (lower). Dual leadership reflecting the two moieties of the community was not uncommon.

After the Incas subjugated new territories, they appointed new *curacas*, *capacs*, and *sinchis* or forced existing ones to swear allegiance to them. They chose these leaders from among local men, unless they suspected them of anti-Inca sentiments, in which case, they appointed men from the royal *ayllus* of Cuzco (Moseley, 1992).

The high society in imperial Cuzco closely reflected this general Andean model. The city of Cuzco was occupied almost exclusively by about a dozen *ayllus* that claimed the first Inca, Manco Capac, as their common ancestor. These *ayllus* were divided into two moieties, *Hanan* (Upper) Cuzco and *Hurin* (Lower) that lived in two different areas of Cuzco (Cobo, 1979). Their emperor, who held the title of Sapa Inca ("Only Inca"), was customarily elected by the leaders of the *ayllus*. He was usually a son or close blood relative of the previous *Sapa Inca*, who often nominated him as his successor. However, the leaders of the Cuzco *ayllus* did not have to accept the Inca's choice and could appoint another man, as long as he came from the Inca's lineage. This probably explains why almost every time a new Inca was selected, there were rival candidates for the post and the new ruler, if he was capable, had to squash plots against him and execute or exile dissenters. Sometimes, as in the case of Viracocha, the reigning Inca supported the losing candidate, which led to further friction or out-and-out civil war. Periods of dual leadership were also common. Thus, Viracocha was co-emperor with his son Urcos and later with his son Inca Yupanque, later known as Pachacutec, who shared power in his later years with his son Tupa Inca Yupanque. Tupa Inca's son, Huayna Capac, who campaigned extensively in the north of his empire, put his cousin in charge of the administration of the empire in Cuzco (Cobo, 1979; Betanzos, 1996; Moseley 1992).

Administrative organization of the population

Although the Incas recognized the various ethnic and kinship groups under their rule, for administrative expediency they also organized them according to a decimal system. Thus, the administrative *ayllu* comprised 100 *pachacas*, or lineages, each headed by a *purej* or family head. Sometimes, the *ayllus* were further subdivided into units of 10 and 50 *pachacas*, whose leader was appointed by the *curaca* of the *ayllu*. Five *ayllus* formed a *pihcapachaca* (500 *pachacas*) led by a *pihcapachaca curaca*. Two *pihcapachacas* or 1,000 *pachacas* formed a *waranka* whose leader was a *waranka curaca*. Ten *warankas* formed one *huno* administered by the *huno curaca* who collected population data from his subordinates and reported directly to the Inca. He was assisted in this work by the *quipucamayocs* (Moseley, 1992; Kauffmann-Doig, 1980).

Territorial organization

Generally speaking, personal property did not exist in the pre-Columbian Andean region. The land belonged to the *ayllu* and the *curaca* allotted a plot (*topo*) to each family. At the death of its holder, a *topo* reverted to the *ayllu*. The territory of the *ayllu*, called *marca*, varied in size, depending on the region and the resources available. In areas with poor rainfall or soils, the *marcas* tended to be large, whereas in fertile valleys, they tended to be smaller. Typically, they occupied various elevations, so that the *ayllu* could exploit various ecological niches. Each *topo* also spread over various elevations, so all the families of the *ayllu* could have equal access to all the ecological niches. When the Incas came to power, they laid claim to all the land in the name of the state and Inti, the sun god, but allowed the *curacas* to continue apportioning the land as they had always done. The size of a *marca* was now large enough to provide 100 families with plots. A variable number of *marcas* formed a sector called a *saya*, and an undetermined number of *sayas* made up a *huamani* or province. These provinces corresponded roughly to the territories of the tribes or city-states conquered by the Incas and retained their old names and capitals. The provinces, in turn, made up the four *suyos* of Tawantinsuyu: Collasuyu, Cuntisuyu, Antisuyu, and Chinchaysuyu (Kauffmann-Doig, 1980).

Social classes

In addition to the *ayllus*, based on kinship ties, Tawantinsuyu society was divided into a pyramidal structure with the Inca at the top. Below the ruler was the aristocracy formed by the *ayllus* of Cuzco. These noblemen were called *orejones* (big ears) by the Spaniards because they wore enormous gold earplugs in their earlobes. It is from this class that the Inca army drew most of its cadre and its elite units as well as its administrators and governors.

The common people were called *mitimacs* (taxpayers) or *runas*. They provided the Incas with the labor and goods necessary to run the empire and the bulk of their army. The lowest class was constituted by the *yanakunas* (servants or slaves) who served the Inca, his relatives and the Cuzco nobility. They were usually prisoners of war or transplanted artisans from the conquered provinces.

The Sapa Inca, who was considered to be the direct descendant of Inti, the sun god, was at the top of the social pyramid. All the land of the empire belonged either to him or to his ancestor, the sun god. The highest-ranking people below him were the sons and daughters of his predecessor, who lived in the compound of the deceased Inca and tended to his needs. Paramount chiefs of kings who had surrendered to the Inca retained their high status, and answered directly to the Sapa Inca. Subsequent generations of deceased Incas lost some status, but still enjoyed a privileged status in Inca society. Members of closely allied tribes enjoyed the same status as the Incas, even when they were transplanted into different parts of the empire as *mitimacs*, whose role was to pacify the locals. Outstanding military leaders and administrators could rise from the ranks of the commoners to this level of society. The bulk of the population of Tawantinsuyu consisted of commoners, who provided the Inca with goods and services. At the bottom of the pyramid were rebellious subjects who were forcibly transplanted from their original homelands, and *yanakunas* who served as personal slaves to the upper classes. All these classes were further subdivided into *ayllus* (clans) grouped into two moieties: Hanan and Hurin. (Chart after Kauffmann-Doig, 1985.)

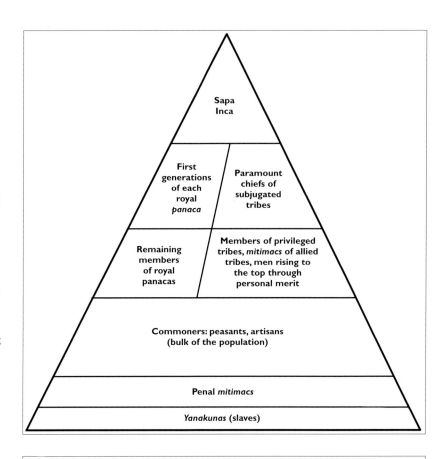

RIGHT **Andean social organization**

In addition to being organized in social classes, Andean societies were organized into kinship groups that relied on each other for help with agricultural chores as well as protection and warfare. The Incas used this social structure to organize their armies.

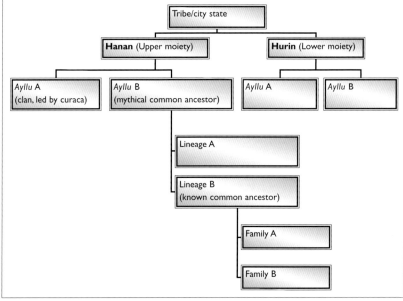

The *mit'a*

The *mit'a* was the name given to the labor obligation owed by one family to the other in the *ayllu* system. With the advent of city-states and state societies in the Andes, it became a common form of taxation. The local *curacas*, *capacs*, and *sinchis* gave the families of the *ayllus* food, textiles, and other goods and

services, and in return they gave a percentage of their labor. If they were skilled artisans, they gave the products of their shops. The most prized items were textiles and ceramics. Gold and silver jewellery and vessels were also highly coveted. The *curacas* stockpiled them in their storehouses and used them to buy influence and power (Moseley, 1992; Kauffmann-Doig, 1980).

The Incas used the *mit'a* in the same way as their predecessors, but devised an elaborate system to stockpile and redistribute the products of the land. In every village and town they built rows of stone *colcas* or well-ventilated storehouses for maize, freeze-dried potatoes and meat, llama wool, textiles, ceramics, arms, and other products. Round *colcas* were for storing maize, square colcas were for storing tubers and other goods. The *colcas*, which stood on high ground so that their contents remained dry, were visible from miles away. They were periodically replenished by the local *curacas*, who collected the goods from the members of their *ayllus*. Before the new crop came in, the *colcas* were emptied and their contents were sent to Cuzco, which was surrounded by warehouses holding incredible amounts of goods. Careful records of crops, goods, and labor days were kept by the *quipucamayocs* (Moseley, 1992; Kauffmann-Doig, 1980).

The *colcas*, located in every regional capital of the empire, served to store food and clothing for the local population in times of crisis; men and women working on public works; and the Inca's armies on the march. The *colcas* in Cuzco supplied not only the noble lineages living there, but also a veritable army of potters, weavers, metalworkers, and other artisans that lived in the periphery of the capital. Whenever the Incas conquered a new city, they sent its best artisans to Cuzco to work for them (Moseley, 1992).

TOP LEFT An Inca envoy in court dress carrying the insignia of his office. The men appointed to such roles were carefully chosen by the Inca. They were usually his close kin – a brother, uncle, or first cousin – and they were completely loyal to him.

TOP RIGHT An engraving by Guamán Poma de Ayala showing the Inca general Aucaruna attacking a *pukara*.

ELOTABO CAPITAN
APOCAMACINGA

yñs se chile

The *mit'a* also supplied the Incas with a vast labor force for all public work, including the construction and maintenance of agricultural terraces, irrigation canals, roads, bridges, *tambos*, *colcas*, palaces, temples, and fortresses. It also supplied a ready supply of conscripts for their armies. The local *curacas* were required to raise work gangs, supervise their work, and report the number of days each person under their authority toiled for the state and the temple. In the case of a road, each *ayllu* was responsible for the section passing through its territory. More ambitious building projects, such as bridges or *tambos*, required the participation of units larger than the *ayllu*. All able-bodied men and women were expected to serve according to their abilities. Only toddlers, the very old, and the infirm were exempt from service. Typically, the *mit'a* consisted of 10 percent of a subject's time. Failure to render the *mit'a* was punishable by death. In exchange for the work, the *curaca* was required to supply his crews textiles, food, *chicha*, and coca leaves from the *colcas*. *Mit'a* service was also accompanied by feasting and drinking to make the work less onerous (Moseley, 1992).

The Inca army

According to Betanzos, Cobo, and Sarmiento de Gamboa, the Incas were able to raise armies of 100,000 men without undue difficulty. Except for the garrisons of some border outposts, these men were not professional soldiers, but *aucak camayocs* (men fit for war) between the age of 25 and 50. Each *ayllu* was expected to supply a predetermined number of men when the call to arms went out and send them out to Cuzco or some other point on the road. Although there was no time limit for military service, the eligible men of each *ayllu* took turns in this service. The men who remained at home tilled the lands and took care of the households of those who were gone (Kauffmann-Doig, 1980; Heath, 1999; Fresco, 2005).

The soldiers were assigned to units of their own kinsmen and were led by officers from their own or a closely related *ayllu* in conjunction with an *orejón* from Cuzco. The men of each unit wore the characteristic dress of their hometown and bore the armament of their region. Thus, the Anti and the Chuncho of the east used bows and arrows, whereas the Wanka carried spears and slings, and the Cuzquenos carried bola stones, clubs, and maces. The soldiers were usually accompanied by their wives and children who served them on their marches (Heath, 1999; Fresco, 2005).

The Incas were also careful to use their troops in familiar terrain. Thus, they seldom committed lowlanders to service in the mountains, where they would suffer from mountain sickness and be a liability rather than an asset. Likewise, they kept the highland troops used to the grasslands of the Altiplano out of the dense forests of the eastern slopes of the Andes where their clubs and maces had little effect against the bows and arrows of the forest tribes (Cobo, 1979; Betanzos, 1996).

The units were organized on a decimal basis, like the civilian administrative units of the empire. It is not known whether the units of the army had specific names, but the titles of the commanders were recorded by the Spanish chroniclers of the 16th century. The lowest two ranks, *chuncacamayocs* and *pihcachuncacamayocs*, were held by local leaders, no doubt the *curacas* of the *ayllus* and of the towns and villages, who were responsible for providing the men with clothing, armament, and supplies. On the road, the soldiers got their supplies from the *colcas*, and either rested in the *tambos* or near them. A huge herd of llamas led by herders followed the army and provided it with meat. It is estimated that the Incas required 10 to 15 llamas per soldier (Betanzos, 1996; Heath 1999; Fresco, 2005).

The elite units consisted of two *huaminca* (veteran) divisions – one from Hanan Cuzco and the other from Hurin Cuzco – whose men were trained as warriors from the age of 14 or 15. Their captains, men who had risen through the ranks and distinguished themselves in action, were called *aucapussak*. Since the rivalry between the two divisions was intense and could escalate into violence at times, they were often kept separate on the march and at rest (Heath, 1999).

The highest-ranking officer in the Inca army, the *aucacunakapu* (chief of soldiers), came from Hanan Cuzco and next highest-ranking ranking officer, the *aucata yachachik apu* (chief in charge of organizing the soldiers), came from Hurin Cuzco. Ian Heath explains the other ranks structure:

> Other senior officers included the *hinantin aucata suyuchak apu* (chief who assigns troops to their proper place), equivalent to a European sergeant-major of that period, and the *Sericac* or quartermaster. The commander of an army in the field, called an *apusquipay*, had an aide called *apusquiprantin*. The *apusquipay* was usually the uncle, brother, or some other close kinsman of the Sapa Inca.

The garrisons of the border outposts in the north and the south, called *arccak sayapayak*, were at first made up of Cuzco *huamincas*. Once the area was pacified, they were replaced with local troops on *mit'a* service, who took turns manning the *pukaras*. However, the commander of the *pukara* was invariably a veteran from the Cuzco area, assisted no doubt by the local *chuncacamayoc* or *pihcachuncacamayocs*. The size of the garrisons depended on the size of the fort. It is estimated that a small border outpost may have been occupied by the smallest unit of the Inca army: ten men and their two commanders. Larger *pukaras* probably held larger units (Fresco, 2005). Early Spanish chroniclers reported that the fortress of Sacsayhuamán at Cuzco held as many as 5,000 men (Frost, 1984).

The building and maintenance of *pukaras*, like every other public work project, was the responsibility of the *curacas* and their *ayllus*. However, it is likely that the Sapa Inca commissioned the design of the fortresses and sent a clay model of it to the *curaca*, who took charge of the construction.

ABOVE An engraving by Guamán Poma de Ayala showing the Inca general Inga Maitac attacking a pukara of the Yungas. The Inca troops are carrying a golden statuette of the Sun God into battle.

Major Inca sites

During the period preceding Inca hegemony the Andean people engaged in a flurry of fortification building, which indicates that competition for limited resources, and warfare, had increased substantially. As they conquered the kingdoms surrounding them, the Incas quickly learned the value of fortifications and added their own to the existing defences or built their own fortified systems to hold their newly conquered territories. Thus, there were few towns in Tawantinsuyu that did not have some type of defences. In the circumstances, it is impossible to cover the entire inventory of Inca fortifications in this volume. The present list, therefore, includes only the most famous sites and some of the most typical of their genre. A complete list would probably require several large volumes.

In must be pointed out that the most common feature in Inca fortifications was the defensive terraces. These resembled the agricultural terraces, but were higher and narrower and were surmounted by parapets, which have for the most part disappeared, leaving only low projections to indicate that they had been there. Another feature common to the Inca fortifications was that they cunningly conformed to the terrain, making the most of the advantages offered by differences in elevations and irregularities of the terrain. In addition, most Inca *pukaras* had three types of functions: administrative, religious, and military. Usually, the administrative buildings, which included warehouses, the religious structures, and the quarters for the troops were located at the top of the hill, at the center of the *pukaras*. The size of these administrative-religious-military complexes varied according to the size and importance of the site (Fresco, 2005).

Starting with Inca Pachacutec, the Incas adopted the strategy of building strongholds in newly subjugated areas in order to maintain control over them. Sometimes, they took over and adapted existing fortifications, at other times they built entire strongholds from scratch.

The Cuzco fortress area

The Cuzco Valley represented the heartland of Tawantinsuyu and it contained their most significant shrines. It was the area that was first subjugated by the Incas of Cuzco and had become so totally integrated into the Inca social fabric that it became the source of their most trusted officers and troops. The Cuzco fortress area included the oldest and probably the least standardized fortifications of the

BELOW LEFT The defensive terraces at Sacsayhuamán near Cuzco with the remaining sections of the parapets.

BELOW RIGHT The foundations of one of the three large towers at Sacsayhuamán. This circular structure had several levels. Some believe it was used as a storage area, administrative center, or even a palace, but there are no accurate records. The Spanish claimed that the Incas had fighting positions on the top and used them to considerable effect during the Spanish attack on the fortress.

TOP LEFT The cyclopean terraces of Sacsayhuamán.

TOP RIGHT A "zigzag" in one of the defensive terraces of Sacsayhuamán, seen from above.

BOTTOM RIGHT The three zigzaging defensive terraces of Sacsayhuamán are said to form the plumage of a hawk's head.

empire. Whatever lessons they learned from building these fortifications, the Incas applied them to the construction of later strongholds.

Sacsayhuamán

Sacsayhuamán was probably the largest and most prestigious fortress of the Incas. Its construction is variously ascribed to Pachacutec or his son Tupa Inca, who decided to defend the capital the way other Andean chieftains defended theirs. Although what remains of it today is quite impressive, its ruins cannot give the visitor an accurate idea of what it looked like at the peak of its existence in 1534. Indeed, it was dismantled stone by stone during the 300 years of colonial rule, as the Spanish plundered it to build their palaces and churches.

One of the best descriptions of Sacsayhuamán in its heyday was by Pedro Sancho, Pizarro's secretary:

On the hill, which is round and very steep on the side facing the city, there is a very beautiful fortress of stone and earth with big windows that look over the city and make it look even more beautiful. There are inside it many apartments and a keep in the middle of it, built in the form of a cube with four or five bodies, placed on top of each other. The rooms and apartments inside it are small and the stones from which it is made are very well cut, and so well fitted to each other that there appears to be no mortar; and the stones are so smooth that they seem to be brushed slabs, with jointure of the type used in Spain, one joint against the other. They have so many rooms and towers that one could not see them all in one day; and the Spaniards who have travelled in Lombardy and other foreign kingdoms say that they have not seen another building like this fortress, nor a stronger castle. Five thousand Spaniards could stay inside: one cannot shoot at it with a cannon, nor mine it because it is located on a cliff.

On the side of the city, which is a steep hill, there is no more than one wall; on the other side, which is less steep, there are three, one higher than other, and the last one, inside, is the highest of all. The most beautiful thing one can see in terms of building in that land are these walls because they are made of stones so large that no one who sees them can say that they were put there by human hands, for they are as big as chunks of mountains and hills. Some are thirty hand-palms high and as wide; others are twenty-five or fifteen palms wide. None is so small that three carts could carry it. These stones are not smooth, but they are very well fitted and joined together.

The Spaniards who see them say that neither the bridge of Segovia, nor any other building Hercules of the Romans built are as worthy of being seen as this one. The city of Tarragona has a few walls made in this style, but they are neither as strong nor as big. These walls make turns so that if one was to shoot at them, one could not make a direct hit but rather a glancing blow from the outside. These walls are made of the same stones, and between one curtain and the other there is earth, and so much of it that three carts abreast could move on top. They are made on three levels in such a manner that where one begins, the other ends. This entire fortress was a depot of armament: clubs, lances, bows, arrows, axes, shields, strong quilted doublets of cotton [cotton armor], and other kinds of weapons, and clothes for the soldiers, collected here from all the lands subject to the Lords of Cuzco. They had many colors: blues, yellows, and brown and many others to paint with; clothes; and a lot of tin and lead and other metals; a lot of silver and some gold; a lot of capes; and quilted doublets for the warriors. [Sancho, 1962: 660]

The fortress was situated to the north of Cuzco, 3km from the central plaza. It is roughly shaped like the stylized falcon head often found on Inca pottery and textiles. As in most Inca fortresses, its walls actually consisted of terraces with massive retaining walls topped by stone parapets. Its three zigzag-shaped northern walls, which face away from the city, are 300m long. The zigzags probably had the same function as bastions in European fortifications, providing flanking defence. However, the wall projections were set closer together than the bastions of European forts of that period because the Incas only had close-range weapons, such as lances, bola stones, slings and hand-thrown stones instead of bows and arrows or guns. The cyclopean blocks of stone that had awed Sancho so much were 9m high, 5m wide, and 4m thick. They came from a nearby granite quarry and each weighed about 360 tons. They were used mainly in the first wall. The two higher walls were made of slightly smaller blocks. Three gates protected the access to the earthen ramps behind the defensive walls (Kaufmann-Doig, 1980; Frost, 1984). As in other *pukaras*, the entrances to Sacsayhuamán may have been protected by stone chicanes and small square towers, which have now disappeared without trace (Fresco, 2005).

The southern wall of Sacsayhuamán was made of smaller stones and overlooked the city. It was not as strong as the other three walls because it stood over a cliff, which provided protection in itself. In the battle for Cuzco in 1536, the Spanish forces opted for scaling the triple wall rather than this cliff with the single wall. In addition to its defensive function, the southern wall of Sacsayhuamán had a religious function, probably similar to the three-windowed wall at Machu Picchu. It is thought that the windows aligned with the sun, the moon and a star or a planet during the solstices and equinoxes, allowing the ruling class of Cuzco to pick the best planting and harvest times for their subjects.

Between 1930 and 1934, Peruvian archaeologist L.E. Valcárcel uncovered the foundations of three round structures in the enclosure on top of the hill. Based on oral tradition he called them *Muyacmarca* (round enclosure), *Sayacmarca* (water enclosure), and *Paucarmarca* (beautiful enclosure). It is thought that these three buildings or towers were probably administrative and religious rather than defensive structures. As Sancho mentioned in his chronicle, Sacsayhuamán also served as a large arms depot that probably supplied the two Hanan Cuzco and the Hurin Cuzco divisions. Sancho also noted that the city of Cuzco was surrounded with numerous warehouses, where enormous amounts of goods, including armaments, were stockpiled. In addition to temples and warehouses, Sacsayhuamán enclosed palaces for the Sapa Inca and the Inca aristocracy because it was supposed to become the last refuge for them in the event that Cuzco ever put under siege. Thus, like most *pukaras*, large and small, Sacsayhuamán combined military, spiritual, and administrative functions, which were inextricably intertwined in Andean culture.

Puka Pukara

Puka Pukara or "Red Fortress," located approximately 7km from Cuzco to the northwest of Sacsayhuamán, guarded the approaches to the capital from the direction of Chinchero and Pisac, and particularly Anta, home of the Incas' arch enemies, the Anti. It was built on a hill overlooking an important crossroad, and was made mostly of local porphyry, the color of which gave it its name. Like most *pukaras*, it had spiraling defensive terraces that had held parapets at one time. Stone chicanes and towers guarded the access to each level. As usual, living quarters, administrative buildings, storehouses, and a shrine occupied the top of the hill. Today, the defensives structures of Puka Pukara are often ignored in favor of the rather uninteresting structures on top.

Tambomachay

Tambomachay is located 1km to the northeast of Puka Pukara. The name of this site derives from two Quechua words: *tambo* or rest stop and *machay* or cave. However, the site contains no caves or structures typical of a *tambo*. It consists mainly of terraces and retaining walls with trapezoidal niches. Some authors have suggested that it might have been a spa of the Incas, since it has two water channels that drain the terraces. However, Kauffmann-Doig has pointed out that its terraces, which are very similar to other defensive terraces, and its proximity to Puka Pukara seem to suggest that the primary function of Tambomachay must have been military. However, as is often the case with Inca structures, it may well have held some religious significance as well.

BELOW LEFT Puka Pukara – the "Red Fortress" – derived its name from the color of the hematite from which it was built. In the photo the enclosure of its religious-administrative-military complex can be seen.

BELOW RIGHT Tambomachay, despite its name, was not a *tambo*; it was an outpost that guarded the approaches to Cuzco together with Puka Pukara.

The fortified complex of Pisac stands on a ridge overlooking the Vilcanota River at a point where it passes through a narrow gorge. This strategic location allowed it to control an important trade route that linked the coast to the highlands. The Inca site grew around a pre-existing village built on a spur of the ridge overlooking a set of semi-circular agricultural terraces. Like most fortified Inca sites, Pisac combined administrative, religious and military functions. Just above the old village **(1)**, the Incas built the Intiwatana ("hitching post of the sun") enclosure **(2)**, which included a temple dedicated to the Sun **(3)**, *colcas* (storage houses), and quarters for the troops. Later they built three more complexes higher on the ridge as well as guard towers and walls to protect the approaches to each of the complexes from the valley floor.

The Sacred Valley fortress area

The "Sacred Valley" of the Incas comprises the stretch of the Vilcanota River that takes on the name of Urubamba as it passes by the eponymous city. On each end, the Sacred Valley is guarded by two of the largest strongholds in Tawantinsuyu: Pisac and Ollantaytambo. The valley not only held religious significance for the Incas, but was also a major trade and communication route leading to Cuzco and its environs, and thus held enormous strategic importance. These, no doubt, were the main reasons why the Incas dedicated so much effort to the construction of the two large administrative-religious-military complexes of Pisac and Ollantaytambo.

Pisac

Situated approximately 60km to the northeast of Cuzco, Pisac guarded a gorge on the Vilcanota River. The original settlement, which probably pre-dated the Incas, overlooked the flood plain on the west side of the river, between two tributaries of the Vilcanota: the Río Quitamayo and Río Chongo. The villagers raised their crops on the flood plain, which was irrigated by a network of canals, and on terraces that fanned out from the outcrop where the original village stood to the bottom of the slope overlooking the Río Chongo. These terraces are flanked by a steep ravine and two more sets of terraces on the eastern slope of the ridge formed by the two streams. In more settled times, when the villagers no longer feared incursions from rival clans, they moved into the river valley, closer to the main road to Cuzco and Urcos. On the ridge above the old village, the Incas built an impressive administrative-religious-military complex that controlled the river and the road in the valley and defended the approaches to Cuzco.

Pisac was by no means a typical *pukara*. It actually consisted of five groups of buildings and other defences that straddled the entire ridge. On the lower elevations, defensive terraces guarded the road and the approaches to the gorge. They were backed by two towers. Further up stood four walled complexes, each at a higher elevation than the other, that encompassed the

BELOW LEFT Another view of Tambomachay.

BELOW RIGHT A view of the old town at Pisac from above.

Pisac

39

TOP LEFT The rear gate at Pisac.

TOP RIGHT This is a guard post on the access trail to Pisac.

BOTTOM LEFT Looking down on the Temple of the Sun complex at Pisac.

usual array of living quarters, storehouses, administrative facilities, and religious buildings. Each of the complexes was accessed through massive gates. A trail linked the village and all the defensive elements to each other. Defensive walls protected this trail at various points where the slope of the ridge was not steep enough to deny access.

Ollantaytambo

Ollantaytambo, located approximately 75km to the northeast of Cuzco in the Urubamba River valley, was the first massive administrative-religious-military complex that guarded the Antisuyu road. It is located at the confluence of the Urubamba and Patachanca rivers, at the intersection of two major trade routes; it lies across the river from the Inca town, to which it was connected by a suspension bridge with massive stone buttresses. Like Sacsayhuamán, this fortified complex probably served as a place of refuge for the local population in case of war. It also served as a royal *tambo* for the Inca and its numerous warehouses stored abundant supplies for the Inca army on the march.

Although the Incas took sole credit for its construction, its sheer size and complexity and the fact that its main defences face Cuzco lead most contemporary Peruvian archaeologists to question that claim. Local oral tradition and even Inca oral history seem to confirm the Peruvians' hypothesis, for they mention fierce battles fought between the original inhabitants and the Incas under the reign of Pachacutec as well as a bloody rebellion led by a general called Ollantay. However, the defences of Ollantaytambo may well have faced Cuzco to protect Vilcabamba and its resources from Altiplano Indians rather than hostile tribes from the Amazon.

According to an Inca legend, the town was named after Ollantay, a general of the Inca army who fell in love with one of Pachacutec's numerous sisters, and was denied her hand due to his non-Inca lineage. The thwarted lover returned to his hometown and incited its inhabitants against Pachacutec. After a protracted siege, the brave general was betrayed by Rumiñawi, an Inca officer, and captured. However, by then Pachacutec had died, and his successor, Tupa Inca, awarded him his beloved's hand in marriage. Ollantay was appointed castellan of the place. It is more likely, however, that Tupa Inca offered Ollantay his sister in marriage in order to forge an alliance with him and end a rebellion that was getting out of hand. When Pachacutec died, Ollantaytambo became part of his *panaca* (estate and household of dead Incas), but, very likely, also continued to serve as a *tambo* and administrative center for subsequent Incas and was continuously reinforced and developed. After the siege of Cuzco in 1536, Ollantaytambo briefly served as Manco Inca's capital.

During Inca times, the approaches to Ollantaytambo along the Urubamba River were covered by *pukaras* at Pachar, Choqana, and Inkapintay to the east, and at Choquequillca and possibly at Wayraqpunku to the west. However, this last *pukara* may have been destroyed when a train station was built there. Another *pukara* at Pumamarka on the Patacancha River guarded the approaches from the north. The administrative-religious-military complex of Ollantaytambo was situated to the west of the town, and probably served as a place of refuge for the local population in case of war. Choqana and Inkapatay were located at opposite ends of a meander of the Urubamba, forcing the enemy to cross the river twice if he wanted to pass through. On top of the ridge of Pinkuklluna, the Incas built a string of small outposts with a good view of the Urubamba as well as the Patacancha river valleys. Any travellers approaching Ollantaytambo could be spotted long before they arrived at their destination (Protzen, 1993). No doubt, the guards employed smoke signals to alert the garrison of the fortress.

The administrative-religious-military complex of Ollantaytambo was situated on a ridge overlooking the town in the valley floor. It was covered by defensive walls on the northwest side, where there were no natural defences to speak of and on the south side, where the hill was not steep enough to provide

RIGHT **Ollantaytambo**

Ollantaytambo is arguably the second most important Inca site after Machu Picchu and it lies at the opposite end of the Sacred Valley from Pisac. The site includes the Temple of Ten Niches **(1)**, and the unfinished Temple of the Sun **(2)**, which comprises a wall of six stones over 13ft high (also shown as an inset). Pinkuklluna ("the mountain of flutes"), which faces the ruins across the Patacancha Valley, features several large storage houses **(3)**. On the "backside" of Ollantaytambo massive walls had to be built to shore up the site. A plan view is also shown here **(4)**.

RIGHT The defenses of the Ollantaytambo area. (Joe Kaufmann)

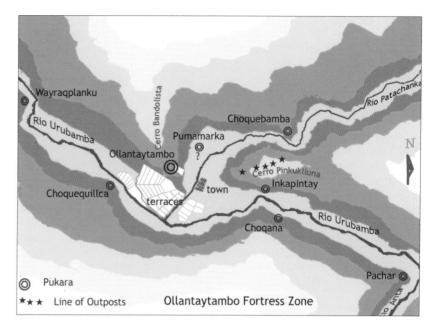

BELOW The access trail and terraces at Ollantaytambo, showing the Temple of Ten Niches in the lower center-right, and the unfinished Temple of the Sun in the center-left.

Ollantaytambo

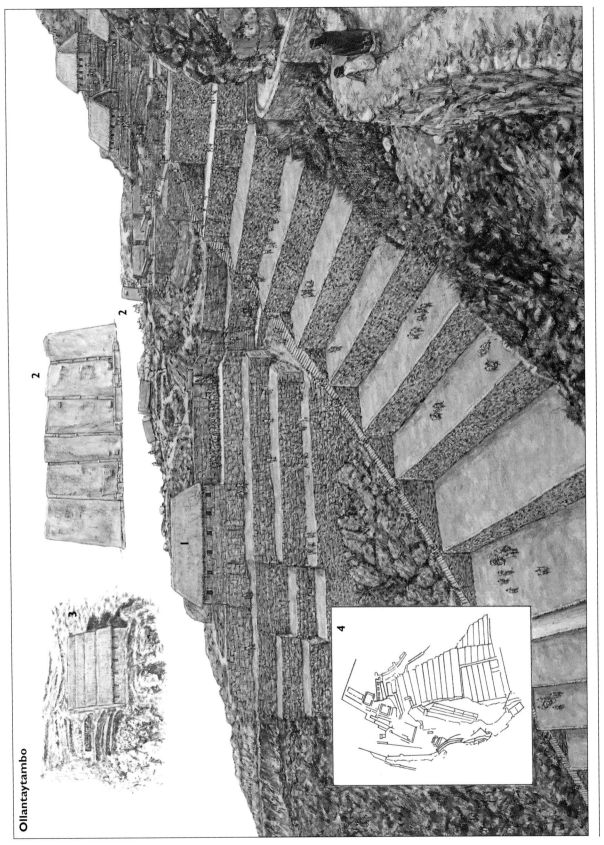

adequate protection. Access from the north-northeast was barred by a formidable barrage of 11 defensive terraces, which no longer have any parapets. However, it is likely that such parapets did exist, as in other Inca sites, and that they were pulled down by the Spaniards who were determined to make Ollantaytambo indefensible. A steep staircase to the south of the terracing allowed access to the enclosure on top of the ridge and to the terraces. It was defended by the T'iyupunktu Gate, which still stands, and a wall, which has been dismantled. It is here that the Spanish expeditionary force led by Pedro Pizarro was defeated in 1536 by the forces of Manco Inca.

The enclosure on top of the hill, which included living quarters, storerooms, and large square rooms, was still unfinished when Francisco Pizarro conquered Peru. The function of this complex is unknown, and it has been speculated, without much evidence, that it might have been a temple dedicated to the sun. However, this complex, which was called Fortaleza (fortress) by the locals and the Spaniards, shows no sign of worship or sacred objects. It is likely, therefore, that it was indeed an unfinished keep built to serve as a refuge for the people of the town in the valley (Kaufmann-Doig, 1980; Frost, 1984; Protzen, 1993).

The Urubamba fortress area

The Antisuyu Road, which linked the Vilcabamba province to Cuzco, was the shortest but the most heavily fortified road of Tawantinsuyu. It served the Vilcabamba province, which bordered the territories of the fierce, bow-and-arrow wielding Amazonian tribes that the Incas had not been able to subjugate. In addition, Vilcabamba was a source of tropical flora and fauna and silver ore, much prized by the Andean Indians, including those dwelling as far as the Pacific coast. Control of the production and/or distribution of tropical fruits, coca leaves, feathers from bright-plumed birds, puma pelts, and silver not only supplied the Incas with much coveted luxuries, but also gave them power over their subjects, who were rewarded for faithful and competent service with these precious gifts. For these reasons, the Incas jealously guarded the Antisuyu Road with a series of *pukaras*. When Manco Inca revolted against the Spaniards, he withdrew into the mountain fastnesses of Vilcabamba precisely because it was so heavily fortified and because the rough terrain made it easy to defend.

Machu Picchu, probably the best-known Inca site, is located on a mountain peak some 110km to the northwest of Cuzco, at 2,700m above sea level in the

Vilcabamba mountain chain. It overlooks the Urubamba River on one side and an Inca trail leading to the site of Choquequirau. It seems to be guarding this road at this point with two other *pukaras*: Huayna Huiñay across the valley, and Huayna Picchu just behind it.

Its architectural style suggests that it was built during the Inca imperial period, and its construction is generally attributed to Inca Pachacutec, who subjugated the region. Since Machu Picchu was unknown to the Spaniards, Peter Frost suggests that it must have been abandoned and forgotten by the time the Spaniards conquered Peru. Frost estimates that the site "was built, occupied, and abandoned in the space of less than one hundred years" (1985: 93). In its heyday, Machu Picchu sheltered as many as 1,000 people housed in 200 habitations.

The function of Machu Picchu has been a subject of contention among archaeologists for many years. Hiram Bingham, who discovered the site in 1911, assumed it was a fortress with military functions because of its location and the presence of walls, a dry moat, and defensive terraces around all the accessible parts. Later archaeologists rejected his theory, favoring instead the idea that Machu Picchu was a religious center. Its location on a mountain peak overlooking the Urubamba River and an important Inca trail seems to support Bingham's theory. Defensive terracing surrounding the settlement on top of the hill is also an indication that Machu Picchu had an important military mission in its heyday. On the other hand, the presence of temples and numerous storerooms indicates that it was also an administrative and religious center, thus combining the three functions, like most Inca *pukaras* and larger fortresses.

On a peak nearby, about one hour's walk away, stands a small outpost called Wayna Picchu, discovered in 1936. Its approaches are covered by "ancient terraces, so inaccessible and so narrow that their value for agricultural purposes would have been negligible," says Frost, adding that "these were probably ornamental gardens" (1984: 103). However, it is unlikely that the Incas would have dedicated much time and effort to building gardens in such an improbable place. These narrow terraces were more likely built to defend the small outpost, which overlooked both the Urubamba River valley and Machu Picchu.

Not far away stands the outpost of Intipata at an elevation of 2,800m. It was discovered in 1941. It consists of 48 terraces, four sets of stairs and 23 enclosures

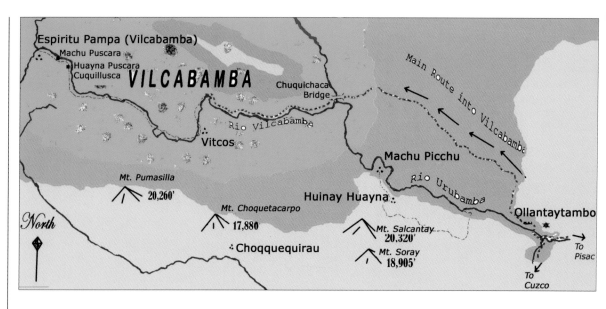

Main Route into Vilcabamba

Espiritu Pampa (Vilcabamba)
Machu Puscara
Huayna Puscara
Cuquillusca
VILCABAMBA
Chuquichaca Bridge
Rio Vilcabamba
Vitcos
Machu Picchu
Rio Urubamba
Mt. Pumasilla
20,260'
Huinay Huayna
Ollantaytambo
Mt. Choquetacarpo
17,880
Mt. Salcantay
20,320'
To Pisac
North
Choqquequirau
Mt. Soray
18,905'
To Cuzco

ABOVE The Vilcabamba fortress area. (Joe Kaufmann)

BELOW Machu Picchu, the last refuge of the Virgins of the Sun.

or *canchas* with trapezoidal niches in the walls, typical of Inca architecture (Kauffmann-Doig, 1980).

Across another valley that opens into the Urubamba and to the southwest of Machu Picchu stands Huayna Huiñay, another larger Inca outpost, also discovered in 1941. This settlement was built on two levels, with intervening terraces. It includes 30 rooms facing to the southeast and to the west and ritual baths. A terrace and some of the walls of the settlement stand over a cliff that drops almost vertically to the valley floor (Kauffmann-Doig, 1980; Frost, 1984).

With its three satellite outposts Huayna Picchu, Huayna Huiñay, and Intipata, Machu Picchu formed a barrier across the valley and protected the trail to the Urubamba River. It was probably built by Inca Pachacutec to secure the territories he had just conquered. As he pushed relentlessly forward, Pachacutec built subsequent lines of fortifications. Machu Picchu remained in the rear, losing its strategic importance, and was abandoned. This strategy seems to be consistent with the methods adopted by Pachacutec's son, Tupa Inca, and grandson, Huayna Capac, in the northern and southern reaches of their empire (Fresco, 2005).

The Vilcabamba fortress area

The fortress area of Vilcabamba is not very well known, since most of its components were only discovered during the 20th century, some as late as 2000. Since they are located in the area called Montaña, they were swallowed up by the tropical mountain vegetation almost as soon as they were abandoned. In some cases, their existence was unknown to the Spaniards; in others, it was forgotten during the colonial period. Clearing an excavation at this site is still ongoing, and many of their peripheral areas, where the defensive terraces and walls are most likely to be, are still shrouded in vegetation.

As Pachacutec moved the borders of his empire further eastward, he built a series of strongholds on the Vilcabamba River, an important tributary of the Urubamba. Going from Ollantaytambo towards the Amazon basin, the first *pukara* in this group is Vitcos, thought to be the last capital and stronghold of the Incas. It stands on the Vilcabamba River, on the main Inca road from Ollantaytambo. Its three-fold mission was to control the region, oversee its economic production and its population, and provide religious services for the locals and the army units passing through the area. Like Machu Picchu and Ollantaytambo, it was surrounded by satellite outposts. These included Yupanca, Llucam and Puquiura to the north, and Huancacalla, to the south. All these sites were strung along the Vilcabamba River. However, since the area has been engulfed by vegetation, the exact number of outposts and their nature is unknown. Recent new finds in the area indicate that there might have been more.

The next group of settlements and fortifications lies further up the Vilcabamba River, near its confluence with a smaller mountain stream. It includes the strongholds of Espíritu Pampa, Vilcabamba the Old, and Marcanay. The Espíritu Pampa group was the easternmost Inca outpost in the Vilcabamba region and stands the closest to the Incas' nemesis, the bow-and-arrow wielding Anti tribes of the Amazon. Like the others, these strongholds were administrative-religious-military complexes.

The coastal fortress area

In the region along the coast of the Pacific, the Incas built few, if any, strongholds of their own mostly because they conquered a series of coastal kingdoms that had already constructed suitable complexes. One of the most powerful of these kingdoms was the Kingdom of Chimú run by warrior-priests who had established their capital at Chan Chan. Apparently Inca Pachacutec was profoundly impressed by the splendor of the Chimú, for he adopted many

ABOVE A view of the Urubamba Valley from the walls of Machu Picchu. The road in the background leading up from the valley floor is a modern one.

47

of their customs and administrative practices. Apart from some minor architectural additions and the construction of an *ushnu* (altar) dedicated to the sun, the Incas left most of the coastal strongholds and outposts intact, incorporating them into their empire.

Tambo Colorado

Tambo Colorado, also known as Pucatambo, Pucallacta or Pucahuasi ("red *tambo*") is situated on the old Inca road, in the Pisco Valley, about 270km to the south of Lima. It was probably a pre-Inca settlement that grew along an important trade route. After the Inca Pachacutec took it over around 1450, he transformed it into a *tambo* where he could rest and re-supply his armies. Apparently, Tambo Colorado played an important role in the wars with the coastal states during the reigns of Pachacutec and Tupa Inca.

Tambo Colorado is made of red adobe bricks, a common construction material in the area. However, it also incorporates architectural elements of the Inca traditions like trapezoidal niches and doorways. It consists of three main sectors built around a trapezoidal plaza and it is intersected by an Inca road that links the coastal highway to the Sierra highway.

Like most Inca settlements of this type, it was an administrative-religious-military complex. The southwestern sector, which is the smallest, stands apart from the other two. It consists of a large enclosure with walls on three sides that opens onto the dry bed of the Pisco River. In the northeast corner, there are several rooms that may have been used for storage.

The southeastern sector is the largest of the three and consists of several abutting buildings and an *ushnu* (altar) in the form of a platform that allows a good view of the valley. The two largest buildings in this complex are actually courtyards surrounded by various rooms. The entire sector is enclosed by a high adobe wall.

The northern sector is a large rectangular building with a single entrance and a central patio surrounded by a maze of small rooms. This building, which is 100m wide and 150m long, stands in a fold of the terrain to the north of the Inca road. It is flanked with two smaller multi-room buildings. At one time, the entire complex was decorated with red, yellow, and white stucco, which can still be seen in patches today.

The road on either side of the plaza was easily defended as it passed between the buildings of the northern and the southeastern sectors. The large plaza probably served as an assembly point for the Incas' armies and as a ceremonial area where the soldiers performed their war dances before they sallied forth to wage war on their enemies (Kauffmann-Doig, 1980).

Paramonga

The "fortress" of Paramonga is located to the north of Lima, on the old coastal road of the Incas, near the settlement of Pativilca. It stands on the banks of the Fortaleza River, less than 1km from the Pacific Ocean. Built between 1200 and 1400 CE, it was an important outpost and worship center on the southern border of the Chimú kingdom. Like most of the fortification of the Andean region, it probably combined administrative, religious, and military functions. In its heyday, it dominated the town, the river, the road, and the fields around it. It was conquered and integrated into the Inca defensive system by Pachacutec, who brought the Chimú kingdom to its knees.

Paramonga is made entirely of adobe and adobe bricks and consists of terraces built around the contours of a hill to form a rough pentagon. Although Hernán Cortés reported seeing five walls in 1532, Paramonga actually consists of four terraces. The administrative and religious buildings stand on the last terrace, surrounded by their own wall, which might have given Pizarro the impression that there were five walls. At the corners of Paramonga, four trapezoidal structures give the complex the appearance of a European bastioned fortification. Seen from the sky, the complex looks like a stylized flame, probably an effect deliberately sought. According to the early Spanish chroniclers, the walls of Paramonga were entirely plastered with brightly colored stucco, lavishly decorated with animal and bird motifs. Today, the plaster is all but gone and large sections of the adobe terraces are crumbling away. Even so, this fortress is still the best-preserved construction in the area.

Paramonga is a fairly typical pre-Colombian fortification of the Peruvian coast. It is reported that a similar administrative-religious-military structure stands at Tumbes, where Francisco Pizarro and his small force first set foot in Tawantinsuyu.

The Quito fortress area

The Quito fortress area in Ecuador was probably the last that the Incas erected and can be mostly attributed to Tupa Inca, the son of Pachacutec, and to his heir, Huayna Capac.

One of the largest *pukaras* in the area was Quitoloma. It stood on a hill overlooking the city of Quito, and could be considered one of the most classical representatives of Inca military architecture. It consisted of three spiralling rings of defensive terraces accessed through gates defended by chicanes and square towers. At its top, stood an *ushnu*, warehouses, and living quarters. It is thought to have been the headquarters of the system of fortifications in the area of Quito because it was not only one of the largest forts, but it also appears to have held an extensive administrative center and large storehouses (Fresco, 2005).

One of the largest groups of *pukaras* in this area was the Pambamarca group, which occupied a ridge of the same name that ran from north to south. It guarded the approaches to Quito and included, among others, the forts of Jambimacbi, Pambamarca, Paccha, Campana, Oljan Tablarumi, Acbupallas, Guachalá, and Bravo.

Antonio Fresco has also identified east-west lines of fortifications at the confluence of the Guayllabamba and Pisque rivers – formed by the *pukaras* of Lulumbamba, Guayllamba, and Pambamarca – and near Lake Yaguarcocha, whose forts were strung up between Aloburo and extended between the ridges of Yanaurco and Cotacachi. It is likely that these lines of outposts were built successively to secure the territories of the Incas as they expanded ever northward (Fresco, 2005).

Machu Picchu
Like most Inca outposts, Machu Picchu was an administrative, religious, and military complex. Although it is widely thought that it was built after the Spanish conquest of the Inca empire, archaeologists now believe that it had been mostly abandoned by the time Pizarro arrived. It probably served as an outpost to subjugate the tribes of the Vilcabamba region. When the Incas had to evacuate Cuzco, they sheltered the Virgins of the Sun here. The Spanish never discovered Machu Picchu, and, after the last of the Virgins died, it was swallowed by the jungle and was not rediscovered until 1911 by the American explorer Bingham.

The Spanish conquest of Tawantinsuyu 1526–72

Francisco Pizarro, a conquistador from the poor region of Extremadura in Spain, went to the Americas to seek fame and wealth and to spread the "true faith." He was with Balboa in 1513 when Hernán Cortés brought the Aztec empire in Mexico under the banner of Spain. Inspired by Cortés, he decided to mount his own expedition along the west coast of South America in 1524, but the rabble he took with him was easily beaten back in coastal Colombia. However, his 1526 expedition laid the groundwork for his discovery and conquest of the Inca empire. His lust for conquest was spurred on when one of his captains ran across a raft carrying Incas with their treasure near the Equator.

Pizarro disembarked at the town of Tumbes on the south side of the Gulf of Guayaquil, which later served as his gateway to the Inca empire. He sent Alfonso Molina to visit the city and Alfonso returned with extravagant stories of riches and impregnable fortifications with eight walls. However, questioning Molina's reliability, he sent Pedro de Candia to verify his claims.

De Candia suited up in full armor, strapped on his sword, and carried his harquebus, which the Indians had heard being fired on one of the ships. After he fired his weapon, the locals, suitably awed, took him on a tour of the city and its defenses. De Candia gave Pizarro a more realistic account of the wealth and defenses of Tumbes: the city only had a triple row of walls and a strong garrison (Betanzos, 1984; Cieza de León, 2001). Built by Tupa Inca, this *pukara* was one of most important coastal fortifications in the northern part of the empire. With fewer than two dozen men, Pizarro did not attempt to overwhelm its large garrison or even storm the powerful fortress.

Encouraged, but too weak to strike, Pizarro sailed south, past the great coastal desert of northern Peru, to the mouth of the Santa River. Here, he learned of a city of gold and silver located in the mountains beyond the coast that was the capital of the worshipers of the sun. He then turned back for Panama, knowing that beyond the Inca city of Tumbes lay an empire with untold riches.

In 1531, Pizarro embarked a large expeditionary force in Panama of 180 men and 36 horses (from Spain) on three ships for the journey south. After he landed at San Mateo Bay in the province of Coaque, north of Tumbes, he moved inland, struck at a small town, and plundered its gold and silver, rousing the locals' wrath in the process. He then headed for Tumbes overland, following the coast. His reputation must have preceded him, for all the villages in his path had been deserted. Pizarro's little band reached the Gulf of Guyaquil in April 1532 (Cieza de León, 2001).

Atahualpa had informed the chiefs of the province not to confront the Spaniards directly and to pretend friendliness, but eliminate those that strayed from the main body (Cieza de León: 117, 2001). At the time, unbeknown to Pizarro, the great civil war between Atahualpa and his half-brother Huascar was in full swing.

Pizarro's force landed on the island of Puna, whose inhabitants, enemies of Tumbes, welcomed them with open arms. Soon, however, the islanders became disenchanted with their guests. Thousands of warriors assaulted Pizarro's force on three sides. The Spaniards created a shield wall from which they struck down the assaulting warriors with sword and pike while their cavalry stood by in support. This time, Pizarro's force consisted of seasoned soldiers well able to take on the enemy. The pike men, harquebusiers, and swordsmen organized in formation easily repelled the enemy while suffering fewer than five dead.

Reinforcements arrived from Nicaragua under the command of Hernando de Soto, possibly another hundred men. Although there is no general agreement on the subject, the expedition included either two or four small cannons known as falconets weighing about 500 lb. each, which were light enough to be transportable in the rough terrain of the Andes.

Once more, Pizarro crossed over to Tumbes, but the wealth he sought there was largely gone. The fortress remained, but the Inca troops had withdrawn to take part in the civil war that raged across the empire. In May 1532, Pizarro set out on his march of conquest, leaving a garrison of 25 men at Tumbes.

On the Chira River, Pizarro founded the town of San Miguel, a typical colonial town surrounded with fortifications, which served as his inland base. On September 24, 1532 Pizarro began his march into the Andes with 177 men, including 65 cavalry. The company included only three harquebusiers and possibly 20 crossbowmen. As they moved up to the Andes, heading towards Cajas, the Spaniards acquired Indian allies to augment their numbers. Their artillery consisted of three harquebusses and possibly two small cannons. Fortunately, the villages en route were devoid of Inca garrisons, which had been called to join in the civil war. Thus, the Spanish force was spared the task of overcoming any fortified town. As Hernando de Soto scouted ahead through the valley, he found a formidable fortress built entirely of cut stone at Huancabamba. From this point on the fortresses were no longer made of sun-dried bricks. Huancabamba (which means "valley of the stone spirit guardians") stood at a crossroads of the main Inca road that led from Santiago (in Chile) to Quito (in Ecuador). De Soto followed the road from Zaran to Huancabamba and to Cajas, a day away. The east-west highway continued on to Jaen in the Amazon region, home of the head-hunting Aguaruna Indians.

In the meantime, Pizarro and 170 men slowly ascended the Andes following the Zana River and crossed the steep and narrow Nancho Gorge where they found a stronghold located on a pass at 12,000ft above sea level. At this point, the Spaniards and their horses must have been struggling to acclimatize to such high altitudes. The Incas, who were well adapted to this environment, chewed on coca leaves to function more effectively. At these heights, the more nimble native warriors would have probably wiped out Pizarro's men. Fortunately for the Spaniards, there were no defenders, the fortress was abandoned, and the road to Cajamarca was open. The descent to the east brought some relief to the European adventurers, especially those suffering from altitude sickness.

Atahualpa, the victor of the recent civil war, was camped at Cajamarca with his army. He sent a gift-bearing emissary, whose likely mission was also to spy on the Spaniards. He was well aware of the strength of the Spaniards. His first informers had apprised him of the number of bearded strangers who claimed to be *viracochas* (gods) and carried "silver wands" (steel swords). However, Atahualpa quickly deduced that these strangers were mere mortals and concluded that the silver wands could not inflict much damage. Atahualpa also learned from his spies that the bearded strangers were accompanied by creatures larger than llamas that were part men and part animal and wielded devastating power. However, he was told, in the evening the two components separated, becoming men and beasts.

As Pizarro and his men marched on Cajamarca, Atahualpa did not attempt to stop him, defend his fortified towns, or use any of the defensive positions on the roads leading into the heart of his empire. His army, which numbered tens of thousands of men, quietly awaited his orders.

As he approached Cajamarca, a city of 7,000 to 10,000 inhabitants, Pizarro formed his troops into three small units and readied to fight, but encountered no resistance. On November 15, 1532 he entered the eerily deserted and silent city. At the end of the main plaza of Cajamarca, there was a stone temple on a platform, which the Spaniards took to be a fortified position. In addition, a three-tiered *pukara* overlooked the city from its perch on a commanding height.

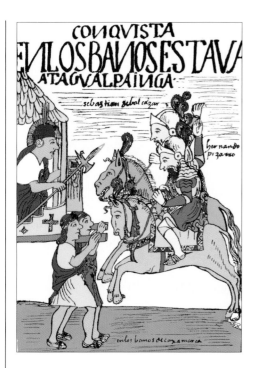

Realizing that the 80,000-strong Inca army could easily overrun his puny force, Pizarro decided to bluff his opponent. Rather then meet his opponents in the open field, he carefully evaluated the defences of Cajamarca in order to take full advantage of them. Meanwhile, he sent de Soto, his brother Hernando, and 35 horsemen to Atahualpa's camp. The Inca's camp was located in a defensive position formed by a small winding stream. It was accessed by means of a wooden bridge guarded by a large contingent. De Soto's cavalry splashed through the shallow stream, bypassing the guard unit, and rode into the camp. Once he found himself face to face with the Inca, de Soto, instead of dismounting and paying his respects to the monarch, pranced his horse almost on top of the sitting Atahualpa. The Inca watched impassively, while some of his entourage flinched and drew back. Through an interpreter, de Soto invited Atahualpa to visit Pizarro at Cajamarca. After the Spaniards left, the Inca ordered everyone executed who had flinched before the Spanish horses (Betanzos, 1996).

The irony of Pizarro's situation was that he had led his little band into the great Inca fortress area in the Andes without encountering much resistance, and now found himself outnumbered, with no direction in which to turn for safety. The possibility of retreat was nil and his only option was to capture the Inca leader. To do this he turned Cajamarca into his own fortified position and prepared to defend the town with guards stationed at all the approaches and on the *pukara* above to watch for the advance of the Incas. William Prescott describes the situation:

On November 16, the scene was set. Pizarro would either take the Inca leader or face certain destruction. Since his small force could not easily defend Cajamarca, he decided to overwhelm his guests inside the town. The plaza … was defended on three sides by low ranges of buildings, consisting of spacious halls with wide doors … opening into the square. In these halls, he stationed his cavalry in two divisions … The infantry he placed in another of the buildings, reserving 20 chosen men to act with himself as occasion might require. [Prescott, 1847: 935]

The Inca arrived with his large armed procession, but stopped and began setting up camp outside the city. Pizarro and his men, anxiously waiting to spring the trap from inside their fortified position, were under heavy strain, especially when they saw the sizable Inca force now encamped in front of them. It was late in the day and Pizarro tried to coax Atahualpa into the city. Surprisingly, the Inca consented, and moved into Cajamarca with his entourage, unarmed. Atahualpa may have been playing a psychological game of his own, relying on the fact the Pizarro was vastly outnumbered in the heart of his empire. As the Inca and his escort entered the town, they found the streets and plaza deserted, with no sign of the Spaniards. Suddenly, a friar emerged from the shadowed doorway, approached him, and tried to convert him to Christianity. As Atahualpa recoiled, Pizarro gave his signal. The falconets boomed and the cavalry of Hernando Pizarro and de Soto burst into the plaza hacking and slicing away. Many Indians were felled and Atahualpa was eventually thrown from his richly decorated litter and seized by Pizarro. The only Spanish casualty was Francisco Pizarro, who was wounded during the massacre. The Inca army dared not

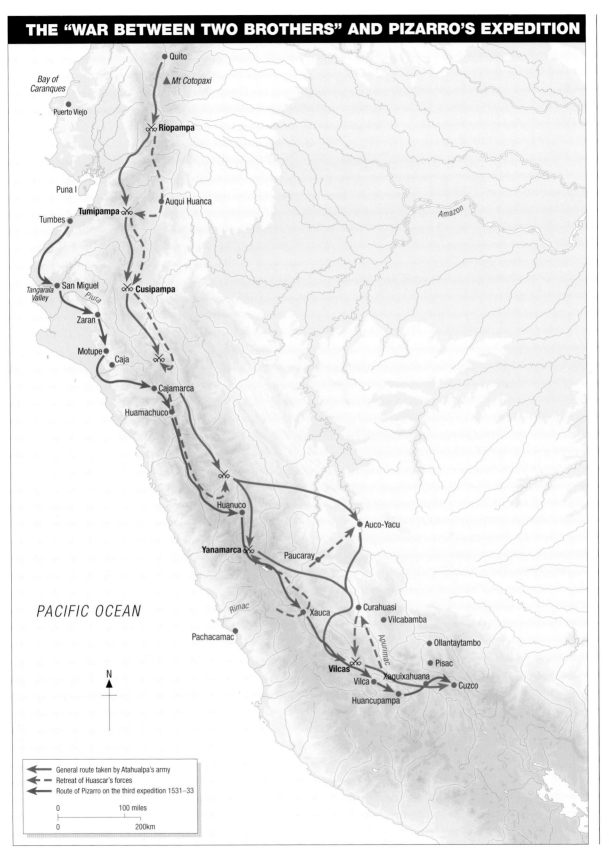

Quito

Bay of
Caranques

▲ Mt Cotopaxi

Puerto Viejo

Riopampa

Puna I

Auqui Huanca

Tumbes

Tumipampa

Tangarala
Valley

San Miguel

Piura

Cusipampa

Amazon

Zaran

Motupe

Caja

Cajamarca

Huamachuco

Huanuco

Auco-Yacu

Yanamarca

Paucaray

PACIFIC OCEAN

Rimac

Xauca

Curahuasi

Vilcabamba

Pachacamac

Ollantaytambo

Apurimac

Pisac

Vilcas

N

Vilca

Xaquixahuana

Cuzco

Huancupampa

Route legend:
— General route taken by Atahualpa's army
--- Retreat of Huascar's forces
— Route of Pizarro on the third expedition 1531–33

0   100 miles
0   200km

attack while its leader was in Pizarro's clutches. In exchange for his freedom, Atahualpa promised his captor two roomfuls of gold and silver. Precious statuettes and vessels flowed in for weeks from all corners of the empire.

However, Pizarro remained in a vulnerable position until Diego de Almagro arrived at San Miguel with 150 soldiers, including 84 cavalry, in December 1532. Almagro joined Pizarro sometime between February and April 1533. Meanwhile, he garnered the support of tribes that held grudges against the Incas and Atahualpa.

Pizarro ordered Atahualpa's execution in July 1533, after which he continued his advance upon Cuzco and his search for wealth. He entered Cuzco on November 15, 1533, one year after arriving in Cajamarca. After unsuccessfully trying to set up a puppet Inca ruler, Pizarro installed Manco Inca, son of Huayna Capac and half-brother of Atahualpa and Huascar, early in 1534. In the meantime, Sebastian Benalcazar, another of Pizarro's captains, marched along the Inca Altiplano highway with 140 men and Indian auxiliaries and entered Quito. Pizarro now dominated all the major centers of the Inca empire.

The siege of Sacsayhuamán, 1536

The Spanish conquistadors strove to repress the natives' religious practices with such ruthlessness that Manco Inca and his followers rebelled against them. In February 1536, thousands of warriors put the Spaniards in Cuzco under siege. A small Spanish garrison stationed at Sacsayhuamán withdrew into the city of Cuzco, allowing Manco Inca's forces to occupy the *pukara*. Manco Inca waited to concentrate his forces before launching a major assault on Cuzco. Since the Spanish cavalry was less effective on sloping ground, he launched an assault from the vicinity of the fortress. The Indian warriors hurled missiles down the hill onto the city of Cuzco. The Inca artillery consisted mainly of fire arrows, red-hot stones wrapped in cotton, and balls of some bituminous substance. The warriors used slings to hurl their projectiles onto the thatch roofs of the city's buildings. Before long, they had set almost the entire city in flames. Cuzco burned for more than a day. By this time, the Inca's warriors had learned how to tackle horsemen. In order to prevent cavalry sorties, they barricaded streets and even dug pits, some with stakes. During the weeks of fighting, the Inca forces took a key bastion of the city walls and held it with their slingers, who pinned down the Spanish. Before long, the Spanish only held the area around the main square. Although they were unable to prevent the destruction, the 190 Spaniards of the garrison and their Indian allies finally managed to repel Manco Inca's force, which probably consisted of over 40,000 men.

Hernando Pizarro, realizing that he needed to retake the Sacsayhuamán fortress above the city, ordered his young brother Juan to take 50 horsemen, break out of the city, maneuver around the enemy, and assault the fortress. To carry out this plan, the Spaniards first had to neutralize the obstacles that blocked their path. To cover Juan Pizarro's sortie, another smaller group of cavalry diverted the besiegers' attention in another direction. Juan Pizarro's force found the passes leading up to the fortress undefended and reached the outer wall without alerting the enemy inside. Under cover of darkness, the Spaniards removed the large stones that blocked the entrance to the stronghold and took the defenders by surprise, aided by the fact that there were no guards. Juan Pizarro and his men rode through the opened gateway of the outer wall and moved toward the second parapet. Soon, the space between the walls swarmed with Inca soldiers hurling missiles at them. Juan Pizarro led the assault, but a jaw wound he had sustained during a previous engagement prevented him from wearing a helmet. Some of the Spaniards were felled despite their armor, but others poured through the breach in the defenses. William Prescott describes what happened next:

The garrison in the fortress hurled down fragments of rock and timber on their heads. Juan Pizarro, still among the foremost, sprang forward on the terrace, cheering on his men by his voice and example; but at this moment he was struck by a large stone on the head, not then protected by his buckler. The dauntless chief still continued to animate his followers by voice, till the terrace was carried, and its miserable defenders were put to the sword. [Prescott, 1847: 1027]

Juan Pizarro died soon after. The next day, as the battle continued to rage, Hernando Pizarro dispatched his last dozen horsemen to reinforce the attack when Manco sent in 5,000 additional warriors. Hernando joined the fray with some foot soldiers and Indian allies as the Spaniards were preparing to take the fortress by escalade. Using scaling ladders, they drove the Inca soldiers from the last walled terrace of the fortress and into the three great towers, one of which was over five stories high, and the remaining buildings. Some of the fiercest fighting of the campaign took place within the fortress. Pizarro ordered a simultaneous assault by escalade on all three towers. They finally overcame the Inca force, slaughtering 1,500 of them in the fortress.

Pizarro left a garrison of 50 Spanish foot soldiers and some Indian allies. Although the Incas tried to retake the fortress, the battle turned against them. By the end of May, even though the siege continued, the position was secure, the situation in Cuzco had improved, and Manco's troops were driven back (Hemming, 1970: 197–203).

Francisco Pizarro, who was in the new city and capital of Lima, learned of the desperate situation in Cuczo in May and sent a relief force. However, mercilessly pelted with boulders on the mountain roads and in narrow defiles, this Spanish contingent was unable to reach Cuzco. Hernando Pizarro, still under siege, managed to sneak out a force of 80 horsemen, 30 foot soldiers, and an unknown number of Indian allies to strike Manco Inca at Ollantaytambo. He took a less used route to approach the town, hoping to take the Inca by surprise only to find that side of Ollantaytambo much more imposing than he had expected:

The palace, or rather fortress, of the Incas stood on a lofty eminence, the steep sides of which, on the quarter where the Spaniards approaches were cut into terraces, defended by strong walls of stone and sunburnt brick. The place was impregnable on this side. On the opposite, it looked towards the Yucay, and the ground descended by a gradual declivity towards the plain through which rolled its deep but narrow current. This was the quarter on which to make the assault.

Crossing the stream without much difficulty, the Spanish commander advanced up the smooth glacis with as little noise as possible. The morning light had hardly broken on the mountains; and Pizarro, as he drew near the outer defences, which as in the fortress of Cuzco, consisted of a stone parapet of great strength drawn around the enclosure, moved quickly forward, confident that the garrison were still buried in sleep … a multitude of dark forms suddenly rose above the rampart … [and] at the same moment the air was darkened with innumerable missiles, stones, javelins, and arrows which fell like a hurricane on the troops. [Prescott, 1847: 1031–32]

Large numbers of slingers and bowmen from the Amazon defended the fortified complex. Twice Pizarro's horsemen tried to regroup and assault the walls, but they were driven away. Next, Pizarro sent an infantry force against the fortress, but had to withdraw under a hail of stones and arrows. Manco Inca had flooded the plain, severely limiting the movements of the Spanish cavalry

RIGHT **Juan Pizarro's assault on Sacsayhuamán**
Juan Pizarro was the half-brother of Francisco and Hernando Pizarro. When Francisco Pizarro left to explore the northwest coast of Peru he left Juan and Hernándo in charge of Cuzco, which they ruled with a rod of iron. In May 1536 Manco Inca led an uprising to overthrow Spanish rule in Cuzco, which led to numerous battles for control of the city and the Inca-held *pukara* of Sacsayhuamán. Juan tried to break the siege of Cuzco by leading an attack on Sacsayhuamán, but he was struck on the head by a stone hurled by an Inca warrior during the assault, and later died of his injuries. The Spanish eventually gained control of the fortress the next day, defeating Manco Inca's force, and lifting the siege.

ABOVE The statue of Francisco Pizarro in the Peruvian capital Lima.

BELOW An engraving by Guamán Poma de Ayala.

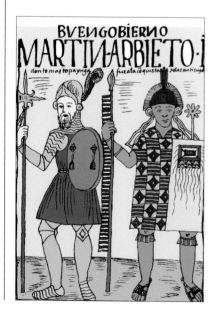

in the muddy ground. Pizarro had no choice but to break off the engagement and retreat. Despite this victory for Manco Inca, his long siege of Cuzco faltered and his chances of success evaporated when Pizarro was able to raid the region for food for the defenders (Hemming, 1970: 213–15). The facts, as related by Juan de Betanzos (1996), seem to indicate that Manco tried to destroy all the towns and stores in the area.

Manco Inca sent one of his generals who had successfully fought the Spanish in the Andes to assault Lima on the coast. Although the city was not heavily fortified, the siege failed because the Spanish cavalry was easily able to break up the assault on the level ground surrounding the city. Finally, after six months, the Indians abandoned the siege. The revolt began to falter even though much of the country still had to be pacified. Finally, reinforcements arrived from Spain and Almagro's expedition returned from Chile (the revolt began when Almagro departed for Chile, leaving a smaller Spanish force in Peru). In November 1536, Alfonso de Alvarado left Lima at the head of 210 infantrymen, 100 cavalry, and 40 crossbowmen. He engaged the enemy in the hinterland and waited for 200 more reinforcements. Thus, with two relief forces coming from two directions, the siege of Cuzco was about to end.

Almagro, who had other ambitions, tried to enlist Manco Inca's cooperation. Instead, the Inca launched an attack with 15,000 of his followers, and was defeated. The Spanish were now too strong to be overcome, so Manco withdrew from his fortress of Ollantaytambo into the mountain fastness of Vilacamba where the dense vegetation was less inviting to the Spaniards. Still, a Spanish force pursued him relentlessly. The Inca ordered the destruction of the road leading through the Urubamba Valley and the great suspension bridge at Chuquichaca. Undeterred, the Spaniards followed him to the town of Vitcos, which they plundered. Once again, Manco Inca escaped their clutches and headed further into the wilderness. It was reported that he established a new city of Vilcabamba in this remote region from which he continued to rule his small kingdom for several years. He was treacherously assassinated by several Spaniards who pretended to be fleeing from Pizarro's wrath after Almagro's rebellion.

Manco had used the Vilcabamba Valley and the surrounding jungle-shrouded mountain range as a defense against further Spanish incursions. The site of his capital of Vilcabamba has not been identified positively, but recently uncovered cities in the area are good candidates. The explorer Hiram Bingham believed it was Machu Picchu, which he discovered in 1911. However, even though this city is located in a remote site and it overlooks the Urubamba River between Ollantaytambo and the Chuquichaca bridge, it is unlikely to have been Manco Inca's refuge – especially since it had probably been abandoned

Juan Pizarro's assault on Sacsayhuamán

by the time Manco Inca withdrew into the jungle fastness. In the mid-1960s, explorer Gene Savoy, after closely examining the site of Espíritu Pampa in the Vilcabamba region, concluded that this must have been the Inca's last refuge. However, during the last decade other possible sites have also been identified as the lost capital.

Manco Inca's great rebellion failed because he was unable to drive the Spanish from fortified positions. However, if the Incas had put up a similar resistance a few years earlier, when Pizarro had first ventured into their lands, they surely would have defeated him.

Tupac Amaru's revolt

In 1569 Tupac Amaru succeeded Manco Inca, and revolted against the Spanish in 1572. The Viceroy dispatched an expedition of 250 Spaniards and 2,000 Indian warriors to put an end to the last Inca stronghold in the valley of Vilcabamba. Tupac Amaru was betrayed by local tribesmen who warned the Spaniards of the ambushes the Inca had prepared for them along the road and mountain passes. The Spaniards rebuilt the key bridge at Chiquichaca and entered the valley, passing through dense jungle to descend into the valley. Here, Tupac Amaru's troops burst upon the Spanish, who were strung out in single file, and engaged them in close hand-to-hand combat. After taking losses, the Spaniards drove them off and advanced to Vitcos. Tupac Amaru's troops continued to withdraw through the jungle toward the city of Vilcabamba, with the Spanish in hot pursuit. A deserter warned the Spaniards that the fort of Huayna Pucara would bar their path. The Incas had prepared defensive positions along the narrow defiles that ran for about three miles before the fort using boulders and rocks. The fort overlooked the exit. Just in front of the fort, they planted numerous palm stakes covered with poisonous liquids, leaving only enough space for single-file progress up to the fort. As at Thermopylae in Greece over 1,500 years before, a traitor caused the downfall of the stronghold. An Indian showed the Spanish force how to scale the heights, and they took the positions where the boulder drops were planned. Next, he led them to a position dominating the fort. The small Spanish artillery pieces finally forced the Incas to retire from it. The Spaniards were able to secure the Vilcabamba region on June 24, 1572, eliminating the last known stronghold of the Incas – but there was no gold or food to reward them. Tupac Amaru escaped, but a small party pursued him into the jungle for more than a hundred miles before capturing him. Thus, the last remnants of Tawantinsuyu were finally overcome.

In November 1780, José Gabriel Condorcanqui, who called himself Tupac Amaru II and claimed to be the legitimate descendant of Tupac Amaru, led another rebellion against the Spaniards. This was the last major revolt to threaten Spanish control of the viceroyalty of Peru. At the head of 6,000 Indians and *mestizos* (those of mixed European and Indian ancestry), he defeated the first major Spanish force he encountered and captured two cannons and several hundred muskets. During the next month, after his force had swelled to 60,000 men and he had acquired 20 cannons, he turned his attention to Cuzco. Only one day before he reached Cuzco, the garrison of the city received a reinforcement of 200 men from Lima. The rebel leader occupied Sacsayhuamán, but, his cannons notwithstanding, he gained no great advantage over the Spaniards in Cuzco. In January, Tupac Amaru launched two attacks against the city, but failed both times. On January 23, 1781 a relief force ended the siege for good. By April, the rebellion was broken and the old Inca fortresses never served again (Romero, 2003: 20–26).

Bibliography

Betanzos, Juan de; Hamilton, Roland; and Buchanan, Dana, *Narrative of the Incas*, University of Texas Press, Austin, 1996.

Brundage, Burr Cartwright, *Empire of the Inca*, University of Oklahoma Press, Norman, 1963.

Brundage, Burr Cartwright, *Lords of Cuzco*, University of Oklahoma Press, Norman, 1967.

Cieza de León, Pedro de, *Descubrimiento y Conquista del Peru*, Dastin, Madrid, 2001.

Cobo, Father Bernabé, *History of the Inca Empire*, University of Texas Press, Austin, 1979.

Cobo, Father Bernabé, *Inca Religion and Customs*, (reprint) University of Texas, Austin, 1990.

Connell, Samuel; Gifford, Chad; Gonzalez, Ana Lucia; and Carpenter, Maureen, "Hard Times in Ecuador: Inka Troubles at Pambamarca," *Antiquity*, Vol. 77, March 2003.

Davies, Nigel, *The Ancient Kingdoms of Peru*, Penguin, London, 1997.

Frost, Peter, *Exploring Cuzco*, 3rd edition, Bradt Enterprises, St. Peter, 1984.

Gamboa, Pedro Sarmiento de, *Historia de los Incas*, Miraguano, Madrid, 2001.

Hagen, Adriana von and Morris, Craig, *The Cities of the Ancient Andes*, Thames and Hudson, 1998.

Hardoy, Jorge, *Urban Planning in Pre-Columbian America*, Studio Vista, London, 1968.

Hartkopf, V., *Técnicas de Construcción Autóctonas del Perú*, USAID, Washington, DC, 1985.

Heath, Ian, *Armies of the Sixteenth Century*, Foundry Books, Guernsey, 1999.

Hemming, John, *The Conquest of the Incas*, HBJ, New York, 1970.

Innes, Hammond, *The Conquistadors*, Knopf, New York, 1969.

Kauffmann-Doig, Federico, *Manual de Arqueologia Peruana*, PEISA, Lima, 1980.

Keatinge, Richard W., *Peruvian Prehistory*, Cambridge University Press, New York, 1988.

McIntyre, Loren, *The Incredible Incas*, National Geographic Society, Washington, 1975.

Metraux, Alfred, *The History of the Incas*, Schocken Books, New York, 1970.

Moseley, Michael E., *The Incas and their Ancestors*, Thames and Hudson, London, 1992.

Poma de Ayala, Felipe Guaman, *Nueva coronica i buen gobierno*, Mexico D.F., 1980.

Prescott, William H., *History of the Conquest of Mexico & History of the Conquest of Peru*, (reprint) Modern Library, New York, 1847.

Protzen, Jean-Pierre, *Inca Architecture and Construction at Ollantaytambo*, Oxford University Press, New York, 1993.

Romero, Javier, *Strategy and Tactics*, No. 214, January/February 2003.

Sancho de la Hoz, Pedro, *Relación de la conquista del Perú escrita por Pedro Sancho secretario de Pizarro*, Madrid, 1962.

Wood, Michael, *Conquistadors*, University of California Press, Los Angeles, 2000.

Internet sites

Finch, Janie and Finch, Rick: www.rutahsa.com/incarch.html

Fresco, Antonio: www.fuerzasarmadasecuador.org

Glossary

aclla	Female appointed to the service of the state, chosen among the prettiest and most talented girls in her neighborhood. Her job was to serve the visitors at the *tambo* and to spin and weave for the state. The most talented *acllas* became Virgins of the Sun.
adobe	Building material consisting of clay and binding materials such as straw, sand, or pebbles.
apu	Chief, or boss.
apusquipay	Commander of an army in the field, usually a close blood relative of the reigning Inca.
apusquiprantin	Aide of the *apusquipay*.
aucak	Soldier, or warrior.
aucacunakapu	Highest ranking officer in the Inca army, literally "Chief of Soldiers".
aucak camayoc	Inductee, literally a "man fit for war," 25–50 years of age.
aucapussak	Captain.
aucata yachachik apu	Second highest ranking officer in the Inca army, literally "Chief in charge of organizing the soldiers," roughly equivalent to a general.
ayllu	Clan or group of lineages that trace their origins to a mythical common ancestor. Under Inca rule, one *ayllu* consisted of 100 *pachacas* or lineages.
aymará	Second most important language in the Andean region.
bamba	Valley.
cacique	Chieftain; a term borrowed by the Spanish from the Carib language.
camayoc	Keeper, guardian.
cancha	Single family settlement or compound surrounded by a protective wall.
capac	Paramount chief, king.
capac ñan	Main road.
chasqui	Messenger, runner.
chuncacamayoc	One of the two lowest ranking officers in the Inca army; he may have led about 100 men.
colca/collca/q'olca	State storehouse.
Coricancha	Temple of the Sun.
Coya	Queen consort, the official wife of the Inca, whose sons were considered the best candidates to succeed the reigning Inca.
cuclla	*Chasqui* hut.
curaca	Chieftain, leader of the *ayllu*.
hanan	"Upper," name given to one of the moieties of Cuzco.
Hinantin aucata suyuchak apu	Literally "Chief who assigns troops to their proper place," equivalent to a European sergeant major of the period.
huaca	Sacred object, often an unusually shaped stone or meteorite worshipped by the Andean Indians.
huaminca	Regiment of veterans from the Cuzco area.
huno	Administrative unit consisting of 10 *warankas*.
hurin	"Lower," name given to one of the moieties of Cuzco.
ichu	Andean grass used in making thatch roofs, ropes and cordage, and the construction of adobe walls.
Inca	Title given to the rulers of Tawantinsuyu.

Inti	Name of the Sun God of the Incas.
lineage	Group of families descended from one known common ancestor.
marca	Territory of an *ayllu* or clan.
mit'a	Tax paid in the form of labor.
mitimac	A taxpayer; often a person transplanted from their territory of origin into an area that needed to be pacified, or in punishment for rebelling against Inca rule (a penal *mitimac*).
moiety	Endogamous group consisting of half of the lineages and/or clans of a tribe or nation.
ñan	Road.
orejón (pl. orejones)	Term used by the Spanish to refer to a nobleman from Cuzco. It means "big ear(s)," which alludes to the custom of wearing large golden earplugs in their earlobes.
pachaca	Lineage or group of several nuclear families with a known common ancestor.
pampa	Field, grassland, pasture.
panaca	The *pachaca* of a deceased Inca and/or his household.
pihcachuncacamayoc	Leader of five *ayllus* in the Inca army; he may have led a unit of 500 men.
pihcapachaca	Inca administrative unit consisting of five *ayllus* or 500 *pachacas*.
pirca	Construction material consisting of a mixture of pebbles and fieldstones held together with a clay-based mortar.
puka	Red.
pukara	Fort or stronghold with defensive terraces.
purej	Leader of a lineage.
quechua	The official language of the Inca Empire.
quichua	A variant of the Quechua language.
quipu	A type of abacus made of knotted strings of different colors and thicknesses on which the Incas kept all the records of their empire, including historical records.
quipucamayoc	Keeper of the *quipu*: a type of accountant and court historian.
runa	The people ruled by the Inca.
Sapa Inca	The "Only Inca".
saya	Territorial sector or administrative unit consisting of several *marcas*.
sericac	Quartermaster in the Inca army.
suyu	Literally "region," the largest territorial administrative unit of the Inca empire.
sinchi	Chief or leader, higher than *capac*.
tambo	Rest house or inn belonging to the state where the Inca and/or his armies could rest and resupply on their marches.
Tawantinsuyu	Quechua name of the Inca Empire, meaning "Four regions of the world."
topo	Plot of land allotted to a nuclear family.
ushnu	Altar or altar platform, almost always found at the center of an Inca *pukara*.
waranka	Inca administrative unit consisting of two *pihcapachacas* or 1,000 *pachacas*.
yanakuna/yanacona	Slave assigned to the household of the Inca or his allies and protégés. They were often prisoners of war that were spared from death because of some outstanding quality.

Index